GENERAL COST STRUCTURE ANALYSIS

Theory and Application to the Banking Industry

GENERAL COST STRUCTURE ANALYSIS

Theory and Application to the Banking Industry

by

Ziad Sarkis
University of Oxford

Kluwer Academic Publishers
Boston/Dordrecht/London

Distributors for North, Central and South America:
Kluwer Academic Publishers
101 Philip Drive
Assinippi Park
Norwell, Massachusetts 02061 USA
Telephone (781) 871-6600
Fax (781) 871-6528
E-Mail <kluwer@wkap.com>

Distributors for all other countries:
Kluwer Academic Publishers Group
Distribution Centre
Post Office Box 322
3300 AH Dordrecht, THE NETHERLANDS
Telephone 31 78 6392 392
Fax 31 78 6546 474
E-Mail <orderdept@wkap.nl>

 Electronic Services <http://www.wkap.nl>

Library of Congress Cataloging-in-Publication Data
Sarkis, Ziad.
    General cost structure analysis : theory and application to the
banking industry / by Ziad Sarkis.
       p.   cm.
    Includes bibliographical references and index.
    ISBN 0-7923-8627-2 (alk. paper)
    1. Banks and banking -- Costs -- Econometric models. 2. Cost
accounting. I. Title.
HG1588.S25   1999
332.1'068'1 -- dc21   99-44532
                                          CIP

Printed on acid-free paper.

Printed in the United States of America

To my family for so much
unwavering encouragement and unconditional support

Contents

Acknowledgments

I wish to express my particular gratitude to: Kenneth Arrow, for his ever kind and patient guidance; Richard Smethurst and John Vickers, who generously opened Oxford's doors to me; Colin Mayer, for his essential counsel and insightful observations; Steve Bond and Bronwyn Hall, to whom I owe a considerable intellectual debt; and Allard Winterink, senior editor at Kluwer Academic Publishers, for his remarkable efficiency.

Naturally, the responsibility for any errors or inaccuracies rests solely with me.

LIST OF FIGURES

LIST OF TABLES

1
Introduction

"Je crus que j'aurais assez des quatre [préceptes] suivants [...]. Le premier était de ne recevoir jamais aucune chose pour vraie que je ne la connusse évidemment être telle [...]. Le second, de diviser chacune des difficultés que j'examinerais en autant de parcelles qu'il se pourrait [...]. Le troisième, de conduire par ordre mes pensées, en commençant par les objets les plus simples [...]. Et le dernier, de faire partout des dénombrements si entiers, et des revues si générales, que je fusse assuré de ne rien omettre [...]."

René Descartes, Discours de la Méthode

The subject of this book is the quantitative analysis of cost structures with a minimum of a priori assumptions on firm technology and on firm behaviour.

From a practical standpoint, the relaxation of the traditional assumption on firm behaviour, that of neo-classical cost minimisation, is particularly motivated by the information technology revolution currently storming through modern economies. It seems indeed less than obvious that firms could, as implied by neo-classical cost minimisation, adjust their factor mixes rapidly enough to keep up with the continuing collapse in the relative price of information technology, especially in economies such as those of Continental Europe where labour shedding is impeded by regulation and other rigidities.

Somewhat improbably, the investigation of a subject of such present interest is in fact best started with analytical frameworks developed for the study of the now defunct Soviet economy. It is indeed in the context of the analysis of Soviet and other socialist economies that previous research has sought to relax the neo-classical cost minimisation assumption while maintaining a flexible specification of firm technology. As discussed in Section 2.1, the traditional neo-classical model, in which firms are assumed to minimise cost with respect to market prices, was replaced with shadow cost models in which minimisation is supposed to occur with respect to shadow prices accounting for possible departures from equilibrium.

But previous research, in keeping with the increasingly systematic use of duality theory in the cost and production literature, adopted cost function based approaches to the estimation of shadow cost models. As it turns out, these approaches necessitate the imposition of rigid ad hoc structures on shadow prices, with the most frequently assumed such structure being the proportionality of shadow and market prices (Section 2.2): *"admittedly a very restrictive assumption"* as Yasushi Toda remarked in his seminal 1976 paper on Soviet manufacturing industries.

This study develops an alternative line of attack building on the primal rather than the dual characterisation of the firm's shadow cost minimisation program. As shown in Section 2.3, the resulting Flexible Cost Model (FCM) is highly conducive to modern panel data techniques and allows for a flexible specification not only of firm technology but also of firm behaviour since shadow prices can be made input-, time- and firm-specific.

With such a high level of flexibility, FCM nests, in an econometric sense, not only the neo-classical model but also a wide range of other models explicitly or implicitly imposing rigid assumptions on allocative inefficiency, such as models requiring shadow prices to be proportional to market prices and quasi-fixed factor (variable cost) models. FCM is also in some sense more flexible than parametric frontier models which require more a priori structure on firm-level technical efficiency.

In fact, FCM needs to assume little more than the existence of a well-behaved production technology to:

- evaluate the neo-classical cost minimisation hypothesis as well as other previously maintained assumptions on the structure of shadow prices;

- characterise the underlying production technology;

- measure the nature, extent and cost consequences of technical and allocative inefficiencies;

- assess how much of an observed difference in cost positions may be due to underlying price, scale, technical efficiency and capacity utilisation effects.

Chapter 3 discusses the empirical aspects of the application of FCM to a panel dataset on several hundred of the largest banking institutions of the G-5 (France, Germany, Japan, United Kingdom, United States) in the period from 1989 to 1996. FCM is shown to be essentially robust to the type of output measurement issues that complicate service sector research in general, and banking research in particular.

The main empirical results are summarised in Chapter 4. In particular, FCM provides new insights as to the existence of scale economies for large banks — an assumption which underlies much of the current wave of bank merger activity. FCM also provides an assessment of the extent of excess labour in the G-5 banking industries, particularly as a consequence of labour market rigidities, and an evaluation of the sources of the current cost advantage of American and British banks in comparison to Continental European banks.

2
Theoretical Framework

This Chapter first exposes a general shadow cost minimisation framework (Section 2.1), and discusses the causes of the restrictions imposed on this framework by previous, duality theory based, empirical work (Section 2.2). It is then remarked that, if a primal perspective is brought to bear, these restrictions are not necessary: neither for the estimation of the production technology and of key efficiency indices (Section 2.3.1), nor for the establishment of a dual characterisation (Sections 2.3.2 and 2.3.3) with a view to studying the comparative statics of factor demand and actual cost (Section 2.3.4).

2.1 Generalised Firm Program

Assume that all firms in a given panel dataset employ well-behaved technologies and minimise unobserved shadow cost with respect to input-, time- and firm-specific shadow prices.

More specifically, assume that firm i at time t solves the program:

$$\min_{\mathbf{x}_{it}} \; \mathbf{s}'_{it}.\mathbf{x}_{it}, \tag{2.1}$$

$$\ni \; : \mathbf{x}_{it} \in U_{f_{it}}(y_{it}) \equiv \left\{ \mathbf{x}_{it} \in \mathbb{R}^n_{*+} \ni: f_{it}(\mathbf{x}_{it}) \geq y_{it} \right\}$$

where:

- $\mathbf{x}_{it} \equiv \left[x^j_{it} \right]^{j=1,..,n}$ is the vector of inputs to the production process with associated market prices (normalised by the price of output) represented by $\mathbf{m}_{it} \equiv \left[m^j_{it} \right]^{j=1,...,n} \in \mathbb{R}^n_{*+}$;

- $y_{it} \in \mathbb{R}_{+*}$ is the output level;

- $\mathbf{s}_{it} \equiv \left[m^j_{it} \exp \lambda^j_{it} \right]^{j=1,..,n}$ is the vector of shadow prices, where the vector $\boldsymbol{\lambda}_{it} \equiv \left[\lambda^j_{it} \right]^{j=1,..,n} \in \mathbb{R}^n$ represents deviations from market prices, with λ^1 conventionally set to 0;

- $f_{it} : \mathbb{R}^n_{*+} \longrightarrow \mathbb{R}_{+*}$ is a firm- and time-specific C^∞ strictly quasi-concave production function, with a strictly positive gradient, non-empty and closed upper-contour sets $U_{f_{it}}(.)$, and a firm- and time-specific C^∞ dual shadow cost function $\widehat{sc}_{it}(\mathbf{s}_{it}, y_{it}) \equiv \mathbf{s}'_{it}.\hat{\mathbf{x}}_{it}(\mathbf{s}_{it}, y_{it})$ where $\hat{\mathbf{x}}_{it}(\mathbf{s}_{it}, y_{it})$ is the unique solution to the firm's program.[1]

Obviously, this general framework encompasses the usual neo-classical model when $\boldsymbol{\lambda}_{it}$ vanishes everywhere, so that shadow prices are equal to market prices and the shadow cost function is equal to the actual cost function.

Further defining $\hat{c}_{it}(\mathbf{m}_{it}, y_{it}, \boldsymbol{\lambda}_{it}) \equiv \mathbf{m}'_{it}.\hat{\mathbf{x}}_{it}(\mathbf{s}_{it}, y_{it})$ as actual cost at market prices, notice that $\hat{\mathbf{x}}_{it}(\mathbf{s}_{it}, y_{it})$ and $\widehat{sc}_{it}(\mathbf{s}_{it}, y_{it})$ are continuous in $\mathbf{s}_{it}$,[2] and that $\widehat{sc}_{it}(\mathbf{s}_{it}, y_{it})$ exhibits all the properties usually

---

[1] Existence is guaranteed by Weierstrass' Theorem and unicity follows from strict quasi-concavity.

[2] Continuity follows directly from the application of the Maximum Theorem to the firm's modified program.

associated with neo-classical cost functions: non-decreasing in s_{it} and y_{it}, concave and homogeneous of degree one in s_{it}.

In this context, the problem examined is that of the estimation, with a minimum of additional structural assumptions, of the λ_{it} allocative efficiency indices and of the $\hat{x}_{it}(s_{it}, y_{it})$ factor demand vector, with the ultimate objective of studying factor demand and actual cost as a function of price and scale as well as technical and allocative efficiency effects.[3]

2.2   Previous Approaches

The fundamental issue here is that, since shadow prices are unobserved, the direct estimation of the shadow cost function is of course impossible.

The solution advocated by Toda (1976), building on the work of Lau and Yotopoulos (1971) in the context of dual profit functions, is to rely on the estimation of the (observed) factor demand and actual cost functions recovered from an application of duality theory to a parametric specification of the shadow cost function.

Indeed, assume that $\hat{sc}_{it}(s_{it}, y_{it})$ can be separated into a core shadow cost function $\hat{sc}(s_{it}, y_{it})$ representing a common underlying production technology and a firm- and time-specific cost-side technical efficiency shift parameter $\varepsilon_{it} \in \mathbb{R}$, so that:

$$\hat{sc}_{it}(s_{it}, y_{it}) = \frac{\hat{sc}(s_{it}, y_{it})}{\exp \varepsilon_{it}} \qquad (2.2)$$

Then, for any functional approximation to $\hat{sc}(s_{it}, y_{it})$,[4] a straightforward application of Shephard's lemma characterises parametrically $\hat{x}_{it}(s_{it}, y_{it}) = \hat{x}(s_{it}, y_{it}, \varepsilon_{it})$ as well as $\hat{c}_{it}(m_{it}, y_{it}, \lambda_{it}) = \hat{c}(m_{it}, y_{it}, \varepsilon_{it}, \lambda_{it})$:

$$\hat{x}(s_{it}, y_{it}, \varepsilon_{it}) = \nabla_s \hat{sc}_{it}|_{s_{it}, y_{it}} = \frac{\nabla_s \hat{sc}|_{s_{it}, y_{it}}}{\exp \varepsilon_{it}} \qquad (2.3)$$

---

[3]The characterisation of $\hat{x}_{it}(s_{it}, y_{it})$ suffices to characterise $\hat{c}_{it}(m_{it}, y_{it}, \lambda_{it})$ since $\hat{c}_{it}(m_{it}, y_{it}, \lambda_{it}) = m'_{it} \cdot \hat{x}_{it}(s_{it}, y_{it})$.

[4]It is in particular possible to choose for $\hat{sc}(s_{it}, y_{it})$ a Diewert-flexible form that could be interpreted as a second-order Taylor series, such as a translog or a generalised Leontief form.

$$\hat{c}\left(\mathbf{m}_{it}, y_{it}, \varepsilon_{it}, \boldsymbol{\lambda}_{it}\right) = \mathbf{m}'_{it}.\hat{\mathbf{x}}_{it}\left(\mathbf{s}_{it}, y_{it}\right) = \frac{\mathbf{m}'_{it}.\nabla_{\mathbf{s}}\hat{sc}|_{\mathbf{s}_{it}, y_{it}}}{\exp \varepsilon_{it}} \tag{2.4}$$

where $\nabla_{\mathbf{s}}\hat{sc}$ denotes the gradient of $\hat{sc}$ with respect to the $\mathbf{s}_{it}$ vector.[5]

Unfortunately, for flexible approximations to $\hat{sc}\left(\mathbf{s}_{it}, y_{it}\right)$, the econometric estimation of (2.3) and (2.4) is impossible unless restrictive assumptions on $\boldsymbol{\lambda}_{it}$ are maintained. As an example, if $\hat{sc}\left(\mathbf{s}_{it}, y_{it}\right)$ is replaced with $\hat{sc}^{tl}\left(\mathbf{s}_{it}, y_{it}\right)$, a translog approximation (subscripts dropped):

$$\hat{sc}^{tl}\left(\mathbf{s}, y\right) \equiv \exp \left(\begin{array}{c} \beta + \beta^y \ln y + \sum_j \beta^j \ln s^j \\ +\beta^{yy} \ln y \ln y + \sum_j \beta^{jj} \ln s^j \ln s^j \\ +\frac{1}{2}\sum_{j\neq k}\sum \beta^{jk} \ln s^j \ln s^k + \sum_j \beta^{yj} \ln y \ln s^j \end{array} \right)$$

where $\beta^{jk} = \beta^{kj}$ for identifiability,[6] then (2.3) and (2.4) yield (subscripts dropped):

$$\hat{\mathbf{x}}\left(\mathbf{s}, y, \varepsilon\right) = \left[\frac{\hat{sc}^{tl}\left(\mathbf{s}, y\right)}{\exp \varepsilon}\right] * $$

$$\left[\begin{array}{c} \frac{1}{m^1 \exp \lambda^1}\left(\begin{array}{c} \beta^1 + 2\beta^{11}\ln m^1 \\ +2\beta^{11}\lambda^1 + \sum_{j\neq 1}\beta^{1j}\ln m^j \\ +\sum_{j\neq 1}\beta^{1j}\lambda^j + \beta^{y1}\ln y \end{array}\right) \\ . \\ . \\ . \\ \frac{1}{m^n \exp \lambda^n}\left(\begin{array}{c} \beta^n + 2\beta^{nn}\ln m^n \\ +2\beta^{nn}\lambda^n + \sum_{j\neq n}\beta^{nj}\ln m^j \\ +\sum_{j\neq n}\beta^{nj}\lambda^j + \beta^{yn}\ln y \end{array}\right) \end{array} \right]$$

---

[5] Throughout this study, $\nabla_{\mathbf{v}}z$ will denote the gradient of the scalar-valued function z with respect to the vector $\mathbf{v}_{it}$.

[6] The curvature and homogeneity conditions of the underlying shadow cost fuction are usually imposed on its approximation. Notice, however, that even if $\hat{sc}^{tl}$ is to be interpreted as a second-order Taylor series approximation around some arbitrary expansion point, the properties of the underlying shadow cost function need only apply at the point of expansion. For techniques imposing curvature conditions at a given expansion point, see Lau (1978).

$$\hat{c}\left(y, \mathbf{m}, \varepsilon, \boldsymbol{\lambda}\right) \;=\; \left[\frac{\widehat{sc}^{tl}\left(\mathbf{s}, y\right)}{\exp \varepsilon}\right] *$$

$$\sum_{k} \frac{1}{\exp \lambda^{k}} \left(\begin{array}{l} \beta^{k} + 2\beta^{kk} \ln m^{k} \\ +2\beta^{kk}\lambda^{k} + \sum_{j\neq k} \beta^{kj} \ln m^{j} \\ + \sum_{j\neq k} \beta^{kj}\lambda^{j} + \beta^{yk} \ln y \end{array} \right)$$

where we recognise expressions which are highly non-linear in the stochastic terms (even after logarithmic transformation) and which are not conducive to econometric estimation.

Some restrictive structure must therefore be imposed on the λ_{it} process — and most previous researchers supposed that λ_{it} is fixed for all i and t, as originally assumed in Lau and Yotopoulos' (1971) study of Indian agriculture and in Toda's (1976) analysis of Soviet manufacturing industries. More recently, Evanoff et al. (1990) maintained this proportionality assumption in their study of large US banks.

One obvious but less than satisfactory way to allow for more flexibility in the specification of λ_{it} would come at the expense of using a rigid specification for the approximation to $\widehat{sc}\left(\mathbf{s}_{it}, y_{it}\right)$. For instance, if the translog form is allowed to degenerate into a Cobb-Douglas function, a straightforward manipulation of the above equations yields a system (of n-1 relative factor cost share equations and a simplified version of the actual cost formula) on which panel data techniques can be applied. More generally, if the chosen functional form satisfies globally the curvature and homogeneity properties of the underlying shadow cost function and is integrable so that its dual production function can be recovered,[7] estimable relations seem to be derivable from (2.3) and (2.4).

An alternative and less restrictive line of attack, which is now exposed, is to return to (2.1), the fundamental program addressed by firms, and build on its primal characterisation.

---

[7] For instance, if the functional form is CES.

2.3   Flexible Cost Model (FCM)

2.3.1   Primal Characterisation

Reconsidering problem (2.1), assume that $f_{it}(\mathbf{x}_{it})$ can be separated into a core production function $f(\mathbf{x}_{it})$ representing a common underlying production technology and a firm- and time-specific production-side technical efficiency shift parameter $\theta_{it} \in \mathbb{R}$, so that assumption (2.2) is replaced with a similar production-side assumption:[8]

$$f_{it}(\mathbf{x}_{it}) = f(\mathbf{x}_{it}) \exp \theta_{it} \tag{2.5}$$

Recalling from Section 2.1 that $\nabla_{\mathbf{x}} f_{it}|_{\mathbf{x}_{it}} \neq 0$ and that the upper contour sets $U_{f_{it}}(.)$ all have interior points,[9] the quasi-concave programming theorems of Arrow-Hurwicz-Uzawa (1961) and Arrow-Enthoven (1961) imply the following necessary and sufficient conditions for $\hat{\mathbf{x}}_{it}$ to be the solution to (2.1):

$$\hat{l}_{it} \left[f(\hat{\mathbf{x}}_{it}) \exp \theta_{it} - y_{it} \right] = 0 \tag{2.6}$$

$$\mathbf{s}_{it} - \hat{l}_{it} \nabla f|_{\hat{\mathbf{x}}_{it}} \exp \theta_{it} = 0 \tag{2.7}$$

$$f(\hat{\mathbf{x}}_{it}) \geq \frac{y_{it}}{\exp \theta_{it}} \tag{2.8}$$

$$\hat{l}_{it} \in \mathbb{R}_+, \hat{\mathbf{x}}_{it} \in \mathbb{R}^n_{+*} \tag{2.9}$$

But, since $\mathbf{s}_{it} > 0$ and $\nabla_{\mathbf{x}} f_{it}|_{\mathbf{x}_{it}} > 0$, $\hat{l}_{it}$ cannot be equal to zero so that the manipulation of (2.6), (2.7), (2.8) and (2.9) yields the following equivalent conditions:

$$g^1(\hat{\mathbf{x}}_{it}, y_{it}, \theta_{it}) \equiv \ln y_{it} - \ln f(\hat{\mathbf{x}}_{it}) - \theta_{it} = 0 \tag{2.10}$$

$$g^j(\hat{\mathbf{x}}_{it}, \mathbf{m}_{it}, y_{it}, \boldsymbol{\lambda}_{it}) \equiv \ln \left(\frac{m^j}{m^1} \right) - \ln \left(\frac{\frac{\partial f}{\partial x^j}|_{\hat{\mathbf{x}}_{it}}}{\frac{\partial f}{\partial x^1}|_{\hat{\mathbf{x}}_{it}}} \right)$$

$$+ \lambda^j_{it} = 0, \ \forall \ j = 2, ..., n \tag{2.11}$$

$$\hat{\mathbf{x}}_{it} \in \mathbb{R}^n_{+*} \tag{2.12}$$

where, even if $\boldsymbol{\lambda}_{it}$ and θ_{it} are endowed with general panel data structures, the presence of simple additive disturbances accommodates

---

[8] Notice that (2.5) is equivalent to (2.2) if f is homothetic.
[9] Because $\nabla_{\mathbf{x}} f_{it}|_{\mathbf{x}_{it}} > 0$.

econometric estimation: either through a single equation estimation of the production function (2.10), or through a joint estimation of the production function and of the central economic relationships in (2.11) which state that the ratios of the marginal products are equal to the ratios of market prices multiplied by the ratios of the corresponding shadow markups or markdowns.

Naturally, while the production coefficients are here assumed fixed, endowing θ_{it} and λ_{it} with general panel data structures allows for considerable input-, time- and firm-level variability; λ_{it} for instance can be specified as the sum of a "group" (e.g., crossed country/year group) deviation of the shadow prices from market prices effect, plus an input-, time- and firm-specific deviation from this "group" deviation.

With such a high level of flexibility in the specification of λ_{it}, the proposed framework nests, in an econometric sense, a wide range of more restrictive models:[10]

- the usual neo-classical model, in which λ_{it} is equated with the null vector;

- other models assuming λ_{it} to be fixed, such as those in the previously mentioned studies of Lau and Yotopoulos (1971), Toda (1976) and Evanoff et al. (1990);

- more generally, models explicitly or implicitly imposing rigid structures on λ_{it} such as the quasi-fixed factor (variable cost) models in Berndt and Morrison (1980) and Berndt and Hesse (1986), which in fact assume that $\lambda_{it}^j = 0$ if j is one of the supposed variable inputs.[11]

In some sense, the proposed approach can also be considered preferable to:

- the line of attack pursued in Reiman's (1994) study of the Hungarian chemicals and mining sectors in which λ_{it} is assumed to be a function of pre-selected exogenous variables — a somewhat ad hoc assumption as, quoting Reiman, "*economic theory*

---

[10] Arguably, many of these more restrictive models, by implicitly imposing more a priori structure on λ_{it} than on θ_{it}, seem to display more confidence in the laws of economics than in the laws of physics.

[11] Input 1 is here conventionally defined as one of the variable inputs.

provides no guidance", neither in the choice of functional form nor in the choice of variables;

- parametric frontier models, such as those discussed in Forsund et al. (1980) and Berger and Humphrey (1997), in which the assumption of one-sided error terms hinders the adoption of flexible panel data structures for θ_{it}.[12]

2.3.2   Dual Characterisation: Globally Regular Functional Forms

With the estimation of λ_{it} and θ_{it} accomplished, the remaining issue is the estimation of $\hat{\mathbf{x}}_{it}(s_{it}, y_{it}) = \hat{\mathbf{x}}(s_{it}, y_{it}, \theta_{it})$, the input demand vector.

This issue is first examined through a special case which occurs when the functional form approximating $f(\mathbf{x}_{it})$ itself satisfies the regularity properties of $f(\mathbf{x}_{it})$ — for instance because the functional form is to be interpreted as the true production function.

Assume that the functional form approximating $f(\mathbf{x}_{it})$ in (2.10) and (2.11) is itself globally strictly quasi-concave, with a strictly positive gradient and non-empty and closed upper-contour sets. In this case, the system defined by (2.10), (2.11) and (2.12) has a unique solution for all legal values of the underlying parameters, so that it fully determines $\hat{\mathbf{x}}(s_{it}, y_{it}, \theta_{it})$.

Consider for example the "Generalised Mean" function defined by:

$$f^{gm}(\mathbf{x}_{it}) \equiv \left[\sum_j a^j \left(x^j \right)^{p^j} \right]^{\frac{1}{p^0}}$$

which nests of course the CES form when $p^j = p^0$, and accepts as a limiting case the Cobb-Douglas function when $p^j \to 0$ and $p^0 \to 0$.[13]

---

[12] For no apparent technical limitation, none of the studies mentioned earlier in this Section seem to have allowed or tested for the presence of firm effects in the technical efficiency residual.

[13] While the proposed function is more flexible than the CES function, it is not Diewert-flexible: a necessary condition for Diewert flexibility is to have $\frac{1}{2}(n+1)(n+2)$ degrees of freedom, while the proposed function only has $(2n+1)$ parameters.

For this "Generalised Mean" function to exhibit the necessary regularity properties,[14] the required restrictions can be shown to be: $a^j > 0$, $p^j < 0$ and $p^0 < 0$.[15]

The Cobb-Douglas limiting case is particularly interesting as it yields simple closed-form expressions. Indeed, in the Cobb-Douglas case, where $f(\mathbf{x}_{it})$ is replaced by:

$$f^{cd}(\mathbf{x}_{it}) \equiv a \prod_j \left(x^j\right)^{\alpha^j} \tag{2.13}$$

with $a > 0$ and $\alpha^j > 0$, (2.10) and (2.11) yield:

$$\ln y_{it} = \ln a + \sum_j \alpha^j \ln \widehat{x}_{it}^j + \theta_{it} \tag{2.14}$$

$$\ln\left(\frac{\alpha^j \widehat{x}_{it}^1}{\alpha^1 \widehat{x}_{it}^j}\right) = \ln\left(\frac{m_{it}^j}{m_{it}^1}\right) + \lambda_{it}^j, \quad \forall j = 2, ..., n \tag{2.15}$$

and, letting $s \equiv \sum_j \alpha^j$, algebraic manipulation of (2.14) and (2.15) provides the unique solution $\widehat{\mathbf{x}}(s_{it}, y_{it}, \theta_{it})$ and the associated actual cost function:

$$\widehat{x}^j(s_{it}, y_{it}, \theta_{it}) = \left(\frac{y_{it}}{a \exp \theta_{it}}\right)^{\frac{1}{s}} \prod_{k \neq j} \left(\frac{\alpha^j s_{it}^k}{\alpha^k s_{it}^j}\right)^{\frac{\alpha^k}{s}}, \quad \forall j = 1, ..., n$$

$$\widehat{c}(y_{it}, \mathbf{m}_{it}, \theta_{it}, \boldsymbol{\lambda}_{it}) = \left(\frac{y_{it}}{a \exp \theta_{it}}\right)^{\frac{1}{s}} *$$
$$\sum_j \left(\frac{(m_{it}^j)^{\frac{\alpha^j}{s}} *}{\prod_{k \neq j}\left[\frac{\alpha^j}{\alpha^k} \exp\left(\frac{\lambda_{it}^k}{-\lambda_{it}^j}\right)\right]^{\frac{\alpha^k}{s}}}\right)$$

[14] Some of these properties (i.e.: global strict quasi-concavity, closed and non-empty upper-contour sets) are unlikely to hold unless they are imposed by the choice of functional form.

[15] The proof of strict quasi-concavity follows from a generalisation of Minkowski's inequality proved in Hardy et al. (1934) and the observation that, under appropriate monotonicity conditions, the composition of a multivariate quasi-concave function with univariate concave functions yields a strictly quasi-concave function (proof omitted).

Naturally, for a less restrictive Generalised Mean function or for other relatively complex (but globally regular) approximations to $f\left(\mathbf{x}_{it}\right)$, $\widehat{\mathbf{x}}\left(\mathbf{s}_{it}, y_{it}, \theta_{it}\right)$ will be impossible to write in closed-form and its characterisation will depend on the resolution through numerical techniques of the n-equation non-linear system defined by (2.10), (2.11) and (2.12).

In the more general case where the approximation to $f\left(\mathbf{x}_{it}\right)$ does not necessarily meet the original regularity conditions,[16] $\widehat{\mathbf{x}}\left(\mathbf{s}_{it}, y_{it}, \theta_{it}\right)$ will be difficult or impossible to characterise from the system composed of (2.10), (2.11) and (2.12);[17] different approaches must therefore be pursued.

2.3.3   Dual Characterisation: General Case

One way to estimate $\widehat{\mathbf{x}}\left(\mathbf{s}_{it}, y_{it}, \theta_{it}\right)$ in the general case would be to return to a parametric shadow cost characterisation of (2.1), but armed with the efficiency indices estimated in Section 2.3.1.

Indeed, with $\boldsymbol{\lambda}_{it}$ now assumed known, so is $\widehat{sc}_{it}\left(\mathbf{s}_{it}, y_{it}\right) = \mathbf{s}_{it}'.\widehat{\mathbf{x}}_{it}\left(\mathbf{s}_{it}, y_{it}\right)$; furthermore, assumption (2.5) implies that:

$$\widehat{sc}_{it}\left(\mathbf{s}_{it}, y_{it}\right) = \widehat{sc}\left(\mathbf{s}_{it}, \frac{y_{it}}{\exp\theta_{it}}\right) \tag{2.16}$$

so that, for any functional approximation to $\widehat{sc}\left(\mathbf{s}_{it}, \frac{y_{it}}{\exp\theta_{it}}\right)$, an application of Shephard's lemma characterises parametrically both $\widehat{\mathbf{x}}_{it}\left(\mathbf{s}_{it}, y_{it}\right) = \widehat{\mathbf{x}}\left(\mathbf{s}_{it}, \frac{y_{it}}{\exp\theta_{it}}\right)$ and $\widehat{c}_{it}\left(\mathbf{m}_{it}, y_{it}, \boldsymbol{\lambda}_{it}\right) = \widehat{c}\left(\mathbf{m}_{it}, \frac{y_{it}}{\exp\theta_{it}}, \boldsymbol{\lambda}_{it}\right)$:

$$\widehat{\mathbf{x}}\left(\mathbf{s}_{it}, \frac{y_{it}}{\exp\theta_{it}}\right) = \nabla_{\mathbf{s}}\widehat{sc}_{it}\big|_{\mathbf{s}_{it}, y_{it}} = \nabla_{\mathbf{s}}\widehat{sc}\big|_{\mathbf{s}_{it}, \frac{y_{it}}{\exp\theta_{it}}} \tag{2.17}$$

$$\begin{aligned}\widehat{c}\left(\mathbf{m}_{it}, \frac{y_{it}}{\exp\theta_{it}}, \boldsymbol{\lambda}_{it}\right) &= \mathbf{m}_{it}'.\widehat{\mathbf{x}}\left(\mathbf{s}_{it}, \frac{y_{it}}{\exp\theta_{it}}\right) \\ &= \mathbf{m}_{it}'.\nabla_{\mathbf{s}}\widehat{sc}\big|_{\mathbf{s}_{it}, \frac{y_{it}}{\exp\theta_{it}}}\end{aligned} \tag{2.18}$$

and, with the estimated values of θ_{it} and $\boldsymbol{\lambda}_{it}$ injected into, for example, (2.16) and (2.17), econometric estimation can proceed.

---

[16] This is in particular the case for a non-degenerate translog form.

[17] The system may indeed have no or several solutions when the exogenous variables diverge from their initial values.

As an example, if $\widehat{sc}\left(s_{it}, \frac{y_{it}}{\exp\theta_{it}}\right)$ is replaced with $\widehat{sc}^{tl}\left(s_{it}, \frac{y_{it}}{\exp\theta_{it}}\right)$, a translog approximation (subscripts dropped):

$$\widehat{sc}^{tl}\left(s, \frac{y}{\exp\theta}\right) \equiv \exp\begin{bmatrix} \psi + \psi^y \ln\left(\frac{y}{\exp\theta}\right) \\ + \sum_j \psi^j \ln s^j \\ +\psi^{yy} \ln\left(\frac{y}{\exp\theta}\right)\ln\left(\frac{y}{\exp\theta}\right) \\ + \sum_j \psi^{jj} \ln s^j \ln s^j \\ +\frac{1}{2}\sum_{j\neq k}\psi^{jk}\ln s^j \ln s^k \\ + \sum_j \psi^{yj}\ln\left(\frac{y}{\exp\theta}\right)\ln s^j \end{bmatrix} \tag{2.19}$$

where $\psi^{jk} = \psi^{kj}$ for identifiability,[18] (2.16) and (2.17) yield the usual cost and cost share equations, but in terms of shadow, not actual cost, and "effective" output (i.e., $\frac{y}{\exp\theta}$):

$$\ln\left[\widehat{sc}\left(s, \frac{y}{\exp\theta}\right)\right] = \psi + \psi^y \ln\left(\frac{y}{\exp\theta}\right) + \sum_j \psi^j \ln s^j$$

$$+\psi^{yy}\ln\left(\frac{y}{\exp\theta}\right)\ln\left(\frac{y}{\exp\theta}\right)$$

$$+\sum_j \psi^{jj}\ln s^j \ln s^j$$

$$+\frac{1}{2}\sum_{j\neq k}\psi^{jk}\ln s^j \ln s^k$$

$$+\sum_j \psi^{yj}\ln\left(\frac{y}{\exp\theta}\right)\ln s^j$$

$$\frac{s^j \widehat{x}^j\left(s, \frac{y}{\exp\theta}\right)}{\widehat{sc}\left(s, \frac{y}{\exp\theta}\right)} = \psi^j + 2\psi^{jj}\ln s^j + \sum_{k\neq j}\psi^{jk}\ln s^k$$

$$+\psi^{yj}\ln\left(\frac{y}{\exp\theta}\right), \qquad \forall j = 1, ..., n$$

and, with the addition of random error terms, econometric estimation allows the characterisation of the factor demand and actual cost functions.

---

[18] As discussed in Section 2.2., the usual curvature and homogeneity conditions may or may not be imposed.

This two-step econometric approach does, however, present two major drawbacks: the need to specify a functional form for $\widehat{sc}\left(s_{it}, \frac{y_{it}}{\exp\theta_{it}}\right)$ and the introduction of an additional layer of econometric noise. A more elegant approach, which circumvents both of these drawbacks, is to return to the primal characterisation of the firm's program and use the Implicit Function Theorem to establish n-th order Taylor series approximations to $\hat{\mathbf{x}}\left(s_{it}, y_{it}, \theta_{it}\right)$ in the neighbourhood of "almost" every point in the dataset.

More specifically, if $\mathbf{l}_{it} \equiv \left[m_{it}^1, ..., m_{it}^n, y_{it}, \theta_{it}, \lambda_{it}^2, ..., \lambda_{it}^n\right]'$ represents the vector of exogenous variables in (2.10) and (2.11), and letting $f_i \equiv \frac{\partial f}{\partial x^i}$ and $f_{ij} \equiv \frac{\partial^2 f}{\partial x^i \partial x^j}$, then since $f(\mathbf{x}_{it})$ is C^∞ the Implicit Function Theorem ensures that (2.10) and (2.11) determine in some neighbourhood of $\mathbf{l}_{it}$ a C^∞ local implicit demand function as long as the matrix:

$$\mathbf{S}_{it} \equiv \left[\nabla_{\hat{\mathbf{x}}} g^1|_{\hat{\mathbf{x}}_{it}, \mathbf{l}_{it}} \cdots \nabla_{\hat{\mathbf{x}}} g^n|_{\hat{\mathbf{x}}_{it}, \mathbf{l}_{it}}\right]$$

$$= \begin{bmatrix} -\frac{f_1}{f}\big|_{\hat{\mathbf{x}}_{it}} & -\frac{f_1 f_{21} - f_2 f_{11}}{f_1 f_2}\big|_{\hat{\mathbf{x}}_{it}} & \cdots & -\frac{f_1 f_{n1} - f_n f_{11}}{f_1 f_n}\big|_{\hat{\mathbf{x}}_{it}} \\ -\frac{f_2}{f}\big|_{\hat{\mathbf{x}}_{it}} & -\frac{f_1 f_{22} - f_2 f_{12}}{f_1 f_2}\big|_{\hat{\mathbf{x}}_{it}} & \cdots & \cdot \\ \cdot & \cdot & \cdots & \cdot \\ \cdot & \cdot & \cdots & \cdot \\ \cdot & \cdot & \cdots & \cdot \\ -\frac{f_n}{f}\big|_{\hat{\mathbf{x}}_{it}} & -\frac{f_1 f_{2n} - f_2 f_{1n}}{f_1 f_2}\big|_{\hat{\mathbf{x}}_{it}} & \cdots & -\frac{f_1 f_{nn} - f_n f_{1n}}{f_1 f_n}\big|_{\hat{\mathbf{x}}_{it}} \end{bmatrix}$$

is non-singular.

But $\mathbf{S}_{it}$ is non-singular at "almost" every point in the dataset as the set on which $\det|\mathbf{S}_{it}| = 0$ has measure zero — as an illustration, consider in $\mathbb{R}^2$ a translog approximation to $f(\mathbf{x}_{it})$ (dropping the subscripts):

$$f^{tl}(\mathbf{x}) = \exp\left(\begin{array}{c} \alpha + \alpha^1 \ln x^1 \\ +\alpha^2 \ln x^2 + \alpha^{11} \ln x^1 \ln x^1 \\ +\alpha^{22} \ln x^2 \ln x^2 + \alpha^{12} \ln x^1 \ln x^2 \end{array}\right)$$

and notice that the necessary and sufficient condition for $\det|\mathbf{S}|$ to vanish is for $\left(\ln x^1, \ln x^2\right)$ to be a root of the expression:

$$\left(\alpha^1 + 2\alpha^{11}\ln x^1 + \alpha^{12}\ln x^2\right)^2 *$$

$$\left[-\alpha^2 + 2\alpha^{22}(1 - \ln x^2) - \alpha^{12}\ln x^1\right]$$

$$-2\alpha^{12}\left(\alpha^2 + 2\alpha^{22}\ln x^2 + \alpha^{12}\ln x^1\right) *$$

$$\left(\alpha^1 + 2\alpha^{11}\ln x^1 + \alpha^{12}\ln x^2\right)$$

$$+\left(\alpha^2 + 2\alpha^{22}\ln x^2 + \alpha^{12}\ln x^1\right)^2 *$$

$$\left[-\alpha^1 + 2\alpha^{11}(1 - \ln x^1) - \alpha^{12}\ln x^2\right]$$

which can be factored into a cubic polynomial in any one of the two variables, so that its set of roots has measure zero.[19]

Given the existence in some neighbourhood of "almost" every l_{it} of this C^∞ implicit demand function, its derivatives can be extracted from (2.10) and (2.11) by repeated applications of the chain rule, and these derivatives can in turn be used to establish n-th order Taylor series approximations to the actual demand function near l_{it}. By repeating this process for every point in the dataset for which $\mathbf{S}_{it}$ is non-singular, it is possible to obtain a characterisation of the demand function as a set of local Taylor series approximations.

For instance, applying once the chain rule to (2.10) and (2.11) allows the computation of the gradients of the local implicit demand function $\hat{\mathbf{x}}_{it}\left(l_{it}\right)$:

$$\left[\nabla_l \widehat{x}_{it}^1|_{l_{it}} \; \cdots \; \nabla_l \widehat{x}_{it}^n|_{l_{it}}\right] = -\mathbf{T}_{it}\cdot[\mathbf{S}_{it}]^{-1}$$

where:

$$\mathbf{T}_{it} \equiv \begin{bmatrix} \nabla_{\mathbf{m}}g^1|_{\hat{\mathbf{x}}_{it},l_{it}} & \nabla_{\mathbf{m}}g^2|_{\hat{\mathbf{x}}_{it},l_{it}} & \cdots & \nabla_{\mathbf{m}}g^n|_{\hat{\mathbf{x}}_{it},l_{it}} \\ \frac{\partial g^1}{\partial y}|_{\hat{\mathbf{x}}_{it},l_{it}} & \frac{\partial g^2}{\partial y}|_{\hat{\mathbf{x}}_{it},l_{it}} & \cdots & \frac{\partial g^n}{\partial y}|_{\hat{\mathbf{x}}_{it},l_{it}} \\ \frac{\partial g^1}{\partial \theta}|_{\hat{\mathbf{x}}_{it},l_{it}} & \frac{\partial g^2}{\partial \theta}|_{\hat{\mathbf{x}}_{it},l_{it}} & \cdots & \frac{\partial g^n}{\partial \theta}|_{\hat{\mathbf{x}}_{it},l_{it}} \\ \nabla_\lambda g^1|_{\hat{\mathbf{x}}_{it},l_{it}} & \nabla_\lambda g^2|_{\hat{\mathbf{x}}_{it},l_{it}} & \cdots & \nabla_\lambda g^n|_{\hat{\mathbf{x}}_{it},l_{it}} \end{bmatrix}$$

---

[19] The roots could be computed by Cardano's method.

$$=\begin{bmatrix} 0 & -\frac{1}{m^1_{it}} & -\frac{1}{m^1_{it}} & -\frac{1}{m^1_{it}} & \cdot & \cdot & \cdot & -\frac{1}{m^1_{it}} \\ 0 & \frac{1}{m^2_{it}} & 0 & 0 & \cdot & \cdot & \cdot & 0 \\ 0 & 0 & \frac{1}{m^3_{it}} & 0 & \cdot & \cdot & \cdot & 0 \\ 0 & 0 & 0 & \frac{1}{m^4_{it}} & \cdot & \cdot & \cdot & 0 \\ 0 & 0 & & 0 & \frac{1}{m^5_{it}} & \cdot & \cdot & 0 \\ 0 & 0 & 0 & & 0 & \cdot & \cdot & 0 \\ 0 & \cdot & \cdot & 0 & & 0 & \cdot & \frac{1}{m^n_{it}} \\ \frac{1}{y_{it}} & 0 & 0 & 0 & 0 & 0\ 0 & 0 \\ -1 & 0 & 0 & 0 & 0 & 0\ 0 & 0 \\ 0 & 1^1 & 0 & \cdot & \cdot & \cdot & \cdot & 0 \\ 0 & 0 & 1^2 & 0 & \cdot & \cdot & \cdot & 0 \\ 0 & 0 & 0 & 1^3 & 0 & \cdot & \cdot & 0 \\ 0 & \cdot & \cdot & 0 & \cdot & \cdot & \cdot & \cdot \\ \cdot & \cdot & \cdot & \cdot & \cdot & \cdot & \cdot & 0 \\ 0 & 0 & 0 & 0 & \cdot & \cdot & 0 & 1^{n-1} \end{bmatrix}$$

These gradients then allow the establishment of a first-order Taylor series approximation to the local demand function at any point $\mathbf{z}$ in the neighbourhood of $\mathbf{l}_{it}$:

$$\widehat{x}^j_{it}(\mathbf{z}) \approx \widehat{x}^j_{it}(\mathbf{l}_{it}) + (\mathbf{z}-\mathbf{l}_{it})'.\nabla_1 \widehat{x}^j_{it}|_{\mathbf{l}_{it}}$$

To what degree should the Taylor expansion be carried out to obtain accurate approximations? While a general answer to this question seems elusive, three powerful consistency tests are available; dropping the subscripts so that $\mathbf{l} = \left[m^1,...,m^n,y,\theta,\lambda^2,...,\lambda^n\right]'$:

- in all cases, $\hat{\mathbf{x}}(\mathbf{z})$ should be a strictly positive vector — this will be considered a regularity condition in empirical applications;

- if $\mathbf{z} = \left[m^1_z,...,m^n_z,y,\theta_z,\lambda^2_z,...,\lambda^n_z\right]'$, i.e. if the output level does not change, then under the additional assumption that f is a valid approximation to the true production function in the neighbourhood of $\hat{\mathbf{x}}(\mathbf{z})$, $f\left[\hat{\mathbf{x}}(\mathbf{z})\right]$ should be approximately equal to y;

- if $z = [m^1, ..., m^n, y, \theta, 0^2, ..., 0^n]'$, i.e. if the only difference is the assumption of market (versus shadow) price minimisation, then the actual cost $\mathbf{m}'.\hat{\mathbf{x}}(z)$ should be less than or equal to $\mathbf{m}'.\hat{\mathbf{x}}(1)$ — this will also be considered a regularity condition in empirical applications.

2.4 Comparative Statics

In what follows, assume that, using the methodology previously exposed, estimates of the θ_{it} and λ_{it} processes have been obtained as well as a satisfactory characterisation of $\hat{\mathbf{x}}(\mathbf{m}_{it}, y_{it}, \theta_{it}, \lambda_{it})$ as a set of first- or higher-order local Taylor series approximations. It is then of course possible to study the comparative statics of factor demand and cost.

In particular, it is possible to estimate for each observation in the dataset an input-specific capacity utilisation rate and an aggregate disequilibrium index:

$$
\begin{aligned}
\varphi_{it}^j &= \varphi^j(\mathbf{m}_{it}, y_{it}, \theta_{it}, \lambda_{it}) \\
&\equiv \frac{\hat{x}^j(\mathbf{m}_{it}, y_{it}, \theta_{it}, 0)}{\hat{x}^j(\mathbf{m}_{it}, y_{it}, \theta_{it}, \lambda_{it})}, \qquad \forall\, j = 1, ..., n
\end{aligned}
$$

$$
\vartheta_{it} \equiv \sqrt{\sum_{j=1}^{n} \left(\varphi_{it}^j - 1\right)^2}
$$

as well as the cost surcharge induced by disequilibrium:

$$
\begin{aligned}
\tau_{it} &= \tau(\mathbf{m}_{it}, y_{it}, \theta_{it}, \lambda_{it}) \\
&\equiv 1 - \frac{\hat{c}(\mathbf{m}_{it}, y_{it}, \theta_{it}, 0)}{\hat{c}(\mathbf{m}_{it}, y_{it}, \theta_{it}, \lambda_{it})} \\
&\approx \ln\left[\frac{\hat{c}(\mathbf{m}_{it}, y_{it}, \theta_{it}, \lambda_{it})}{\hat{c}(\mathbf{m}_{it}, y_{it}, \theta_{it}, 0)}\right]
\end{aligned}
$$

Furthermore, define the cost position as the cost/income ratio:

$$
\xi_{it} = \xi(\mathbf{m}_{it}, y_{it}, \theta_{it}, \lambda_{it}) \equiv \frac{\mathbf{m}_{it}'.\hat{\mathbf{x}}(\mathbf{m}_{it}, y_{it}, \theta_{it}, \lambda_{it})}{y_{it}} \tag{2.20}
$$

and let δ_b^a be the observed cost position difference between observations $\mathbf{a} \equiv [\mathbf{m}_a, y_a, \theta_a, \boldsymbol{\lambda}_a]$ and $\mathbf{b} \equiv [\mathbf{m}_b, y_b, \theta_b, \boldsymbol{\lambda}_b]$:

$$\delta_b^a \equiv \xi|_{\mathbf{a}} - \xi|_{\mathbf{b}} \tag{2.21}$$

Now, $\boldsymbol{\nabla}\xi|_{\mathbf{a}}$ and $\boldsymbol{\nabla}\xi|_{\mathbf{b}}$, as well as higher-order derivatives, can be obtained by differentiating (2.20) and it is possible to write n-th order Taylor approximations to $\xi|_{\mathbf{a}}$ near $\xi|_{\mathbf{b}}$ and to $\xi|_{\mathbf{b}}$ near $\xi|_{\mathbf{a}}$:

$$\xi|_{\mathbf{a}} \approx \xi|_{\mathbf{b}} + (\mathbf{a} - \mathbf{b})' . \boldsymbol{\nabla}\xi|_{\mathbf{b}} + \ldots \tag{2.22}$$

$$\xi|_{\mathbf{b}} \approx \xi|_{\mathbf{a}} + (\mathbf{b} - \mathbf{a})' . \boldsymbol{\nabla}\xi|_{\mathbf{a}} + \ldots \tag{2.23}$$

where the dots represent possible higher-order terms.

Finally, subtracting (2.23) from (2.22) yields:

$$\delta_b^a = \xi|_{\mathbf{a}} - \xi|_{\mathbf{b}} \approx \frac{1}{2}(\mathbf{a} - \mathbf{b})' . [\boldsymbol{\nabla}\xi|_{\mathbf{a}} + \boldsymbol{\nabla}\xi|_{\mathbf{b}}] + \ldots \tag{2.24}$$

which expresses the observed cost differential as a symmetric function of underlying price, scale, technical efficiency and disequilibrium effects.

3
Empirical Modelling

Turning to the implementation of FCM on an international banking dataset, Section 3.1 summarises the main empirical questions and their context. Section 3.2 discusses the measurement difficulties that must be confronted in banking research, especially in a multinational setting, while Section 3.3 describes the dataset constructed for this study. Finally, Section 3.4 presents the parametric specification, the main econometric issues, the chosen estimation techniques, and the dual characterisation relations that emerge from the chosen parametric specification.

3.1 Empirical Context and Issues

The study of the G-5 banking industries could be motivated solely by the considerable importance of these industries to the G-5 economies.[1] This importance largely explains the voluminous (although essentially US-focused) body of literature on bank cost and production, starting with the early contributions of Benston (1965) and Bell and Murphy (1968).[2]

But the G-5 banking industries are also worth studying because of their exemplarity. Banking can indeed be considered a prototypical service activity: the technology of banking is hardly specific and the same fundamental information-processing tasks, historically paper-based, are at the core of insurance, of government and of other clerical activities conducted throughout a modern economy. What can be learned about the technology and cost structure of banking might therefore provide insights into the possible evolution of considerable portions of the G-5 economies.

Furthermore, beyond these general considerations, three intriguing characteristics of the G-5 banking industries in the 1989-1996 period deserve special examination.

Firstly, because of the continued decline in the price of (information) technology relative to that of labour, the factor mix of the G-5 banks has dramatically evolved in favour of technology. This evolution can be traced back at least to the early 1980s, when most banks started to spend massively on technology. By the late 1980s, bank employment had peaked in every G-5 banking industry,[3] while technology investments continued to rapidly increase.[4] It is often suspected that the process of technology-for-labour substitution, while swift, may not have been swift enough to keep up with the dramatic

---

[1] In the UK in 1996, for instance, commercial banks alone numbered 348,000 employees and their operating expenses amounted to £23.6 billion. [The data sources used for these and other facts presented in this Section are Carrington et al. (1997) and the FDIC.]

[2] For a general review of the bank cost literature, see Gilbert (1984) or Kolari and Zardkoohi (1987).

[3] The levelling of banking employment has been compared to the peaking in employment for other industries transformed by automation in the 20th century: for farming ~1910s, for steel and motor vehicles ~1950s.

[4] In the United States, for instance, where banking employment peaked at ~1.5 million employees as early as 1986, technology spending increased from ~$14 billion in 1989 to ~$20 billion in 1996.

decline in the relative price of technology, especially in Continental Europe where labour costs have been high and labour shedding has been hindered by regulation and unionisation. There is but a dearth of formal research on this phenomenon: with the previously mentioned exception of Evanoff et al. (1990), prior bank studies have mostly relied on neo-classical or other restrictive cost models.[5]

Secondly, a remarkable wave of major merger activity has been unfolding in the G-5 banking industries, especially in the United States where the number of banks is now ~10,000, versus ~14,000 in 1986, and where the top ten banks currently account for 44% of assets, versus 28% in 1985. In virtually all cases, merging banks have forecasted significant scale economies — although the conclusions of previous research have been mixed with respect to the existence of scale effects in banking: while most studies have found scale economies to be fully exhausted at very low output levels,[6] other ones such as those by Shaffer (1984), Hunter and Timme (1986;1988;1992) and Evanoff et al. (1990) have pointed to significant scale economies for large banks.[7]

Thirdly, American and British banks have operated in the 1989-1996 period with very competitive cost positions in comparison to similar-sized French, German and, to some extent, Japanese banks. This cost performance gap may have been due to labour market rigidities, which may have impeded the adjustment of the factor mix of French and German banks. This gap might also have reflected price effects, since wage rates in France and Germany have remained relatively high throughout the period under consideration, or technical efficiency effects: Continental European banks are not generally believed to be at the forefront of management practice.

In this context, the current study proposes to examine the following empirical questions:

---

[5]This may be due to the focus of most previous studies on the US banking industry, which is the one a priori most likely to be operating close to optimal capacity levels.

[6]Consider for instance Benston et al. (1982), Berger et al. (1987), Gilligan and Smirlock (1984) and Gilligan et al. (1984).

[7]In some cases, recent mergers have also been justified by an expectation of realising scope economies (e.g., for the Morgan Stanley/Dean Witter merger) or gaining market power in a context of generally declining margins (especially for in-market transactions such as the merger between New York-based Chase Manhattan Bank and Chemical Bank).

- Has the process of technology-for-labour substitution been optimal? Does FCM account more accurately than neo-classical and previous shadow cost models for the behaviour of G-5 banks in the 1989-1996 period?

- Does FCM point to the existence of significant scale economies for large banks? More generally, what is the pattern of scale effects in banking?

- What has been the extent of sub-optimal capacity utilisation? Have there been differences between countries or between bank types? What has been the impact of labour market rigidities in France and in Germany on the degree of disequilibrium?

- All in all, what may have been the contribution of each underlying effect (price, scale, technical efficiency, disequilibrium) to the performance gap between, on the one hand, American and British banks and, on the other hand, French and German banks?

3.2   Output and Input Measurement

This study must confront the difficult measurement issues that complicate banking research, especially in a multi-national context in which it is necessary to rely on accounting data sources.[8]

Since FCM assumes a one-dimensional production function, a first issue relates to the validity of a one-dimensional output aggregate in the multi-product setting of the banking industry. One way to rationalise the validity of such an aggregate is to argue that banking products, while differentiated in a marketing sense, actually require from an operational standpoint comparable types of elementary information processing activities so that an output aggregate can be meaningfully defined as the properly normalised sum, across products, of these elementary information processing activities.[9]

---

[8] There is no British, French, German or Japanese equivalent to the Functional Cost Analysis (FCA) program run in the United States by the Federal Reserve System.

[9] For example, if a bank clears in a given year 500,000 checks and examines 40,000 loan applications, the idea here would be to consider that examining a loan application is equivalent in work load terms to (for example) clearing 50 checks and use this "product

A second issue is linked to the unobservability of such an output aggregate.[10] This problem can be circumvented by noticing that the value of output can be estimated from accounting data sources and that FCM is in fact essentially robust to the replacement of output with its value. Indeed, careful examination of Section 2.3 shows that replacing output with its value:

- would not change the estimated production function parameters in (2.10) and (2.11), as long as econometric estimation is indeed conducted in logarithms and output prices (which are latent)[11] can be assumed to follow a stochastic specification similar to that of θ_{it};[12]

- would hence have no impact on the estimation of the allocative efficiency indices, nor on the characterisation of the production technology;

- would not hinder the estimation of factor demand and actual cost derivatives if they are taken with respect to the logarithms of prices, the logarithm of output, θ_{it} and λ_{it};[13]

- would therefore not impede the measurement of input-specific capacity utilisation, aggregate disequilibrium or the corresponding cost surcharge.[14]

Replacing output with its value would however generate two material issues:

---

equivalency ratio" to define a one-dimensional output aggregate, normalised in units of checks cleared, of 2,500,000 (500,000 plus 40,000 times 50). Conceptually, this approach could be extended to cover the number of deposit accounts monitored, the number of electronic payments, etc...

[10] The "product equivalency ratios" are difficult to estimate. Also, while a few banks do provide some transaction processing statistics, the vast majority does not.

[11] Output price is of course defined as the value of output divided by the latent output aggregate, so that differences in output prices could be due to differences in product price levels and/or to differences in product mixes.

[12] The estimation of the shadow cost function in the two-step econometric approach discussed in Section 2.3.3. would not be impacted either since $\left(\frac{y_{it}}{\exp\theta_{it}}\right)$ would not change. Notice however that replacing output with its value, or more generally measuring output with error, would generate estimation problems for both the traditional shadow cost approaches discussed in Section 2.2. and the neo-classical cost approach.

[13] It is critical here to use the logarithms of prices and output, and not their levels.

[14] If the production function is specified to be Cobb-Douglas as in (2.13), the same line of reasoning can be followed for inputs, and FCM is essentially robust to the replacement of inputs with their values.

- the estimation of the levels of the θ_{it} indices would be unreliable, since the production function residuals would include unobserved output prices; however, the difference in the technical efficiency levels between two observations could still be measured by the difference in the corresponding production function residuals if the two observations can be assumed to involve the same latent output price;

- accounting for general differences in cost positions, as proposed in Section 2.3.4, would of course be problematic, simply because it would in general be impossible to measure the relevant differences in (the logarithm of) output, in (the logarithms of) prices and in the level of θ_{it} — again, however, this issue vanishes if the same output prices are assumed.

Consequently, since output was replaced in this study by its value, technical efficiency comparisons and general cost difference accounting analyses will be valid only for observations with identical output prices (i.e., identical product price levels and identical product mixes).

With respect to inputs, the need to rely on accounting data was also constraining. Banks were assumed to consume only two core inputs: labour and technology; the other inputs (real estate, etc.) were considered overhead that increases the effective prices of the two core inputs.

While most previous research employed stock measures of capital, this study adopted a flow measure of technology as multi-national accounting data sources allow the identification of neither the technology stock (in the balance sheets) nor the cost of outsourced technology (in the income statements).

3.3   Dataset

An unbalanced panel dataset, based mostly on accounting sources, was built for 514 of the largest banks in the G-5 (France, Germany, Japan, United Kingdom and United States) in the 1989-1996 period. While all the banks in the sample are essentially retail banks,[15] vir-

---

[15] Across the entire sample, customer & short-term funding and customer loans respectively represent 75% and 60% of the balance sheet.

tually all do have some kind of a presence in wholesale markets. For each bank in each year, the following fields were constructed: output, price of output, price of labour, price of technology, labour and technology.

More specifically, output was defined as total revenues in local currency (net interest income plus other income),[16] retrieved from Bankscope, a database of bank financial statements, converted to current US dollars at the relevant PPP exchange rate (source: OECD) and deflated to 1996 levels with the US GDP deflator (source: OECD).

The price of output was correspondingly defined as total revenues in local currency (from Bankscope) divided by output, as defined above, or equivalently as the multiplication of the relevant PPP exchange rate with the relevant US GDP deflator.

The price of labour, expressed in local currency per employee, was estimated by:

- the average wage, in local currency, in the banking industry of the relevant country in the corresponding year (estimated for France, Japan, the United Kingdom and the United States from OECD data, and for Germany from the annual reports of Bayerische Vereinsbank, Commerzbank, Deutsche Bank and Dresdner Bank) multiplied by:

- an average overhead gross-up rate on labour, technology and technology-related expenses for banks; this rate accounts for occupancy, office supplies, travel and other miscellaneous costs (source: Mitchell Madison Group).[17]

The price of technology, expressed in local currency per MIPS, was estimated by:

---

[16]"Total assets", frequently used in national studies as a proxy for output, proves to be an inconvenient metric in a multi-national context because of the considerable cross-country differences in the level of inter-bank business and because of the difficulty of consistently removing this business from reported balance sheets. Also, to account for different degrees of risk taking, risk-adjusted definitions of output were tested (e.g.: total revenues minus loan-loss provisions), but did not yield significantly different econometric results; most accounting provisions indeed occur ex-post and are therefore not timed to coincide with the relevant revenue inflows: this issue is unlikely to be resolved until banks upgrade their risk management infrastructures and build RAROC-type reporting systems.

[17]I wish to thank Jean-Paul Ndong, from the Mitchell Madison Group, for his very kind assistance.

- the average acquisition price per MIPS for IBM mainframes in the relevant year in the United States in US dollars, multiplied by:

- the relevant PPP exchange rate (source: OECD as previously), multiplied by:

- an average yearly depreciation rate for mainframes and servers provided by DMC, a company specialising in the mark-to-market valuation of computers, multiplied by:

- an average overhead gross-up rate on core technology expenses to account for technology-related costs (software, maintenance), multiplied by:

- the average overhead gross-up rate on labour, technology and technology-related expenses previously discussed.

Labour, expressed in number of employees, was estimated by total wage costs (source: Bankscope) divided by the relevant average wage, as defined previously.

Technology, expressed in MIPS, was estimated by total operating costs in local currency (excluding loan loss provisions), retrieved from Bankscope, minus "loaded" staff costs in local currency (i.e., labour multiplied by price of labour) to obtain total technology and technology-related expenses, divided by the price of technology.

For all country/year/size sub-samples,[18] the dataset thus constructed provides some minimum coverage,[19] and is generally consistent with the elements discussed in Section 3.1:

---

[18] Throughout this study, three classes of bank sizes are considered: "small" banks with less than 4,000 employees, "medium-sized" banks with 4,000-20,000 employees and "large" banks with more than 20,000 employees. Size classes were defined in terms of number of employees and not output levels because of possible output measurement error.

[19] Remark however in the first table presented in the Appendix that most of the 2,778 observations are in fact on American and Japanese banks, on smaller banks and in the period 1992-1995.

- the price of labour is generally increasing, and is significantly higher in France and in Germany than in the United Kingdom and in the United States (Figure 3.1)...;

- ...while the price of technology dramatically drops throughout the period under consideration (Figure 3.2);[20]

- consequently, the labour/technology ratios also drops, as illustrated in Figure 3.3;

- despite the intensity of current merger activity, the existence of scale economies for large banks appears questionable: for instance, a comparison of cost/income ratios and bank sizes seems to indicate scale neutrality for banks with more than ~10,000 employees and scale diseconomies for smaller banks (Figure 3.4);

- for banks of comparable sizes, cost/income ratios in the 1989-1996 period are generally higher for French and German banks, and to a lesser extent Japanese banks,[21] than for British and American banks as illustrated in Table 3.1 for 1996.

---

[20]Notice from the technology price computation that, given data limitations, it was not possible to obtain different technology price estimates for different countries (i.e. beyond PPP-induced differences).

[21]1996 was an exceptional year for Japanese banks which, benefiting from the decline in interest rates initiated in 1995, earned large returns on their bond portfolios, on trading activities and on balance sheet lending.

FIGURE 3.1. Evolution of price of labour

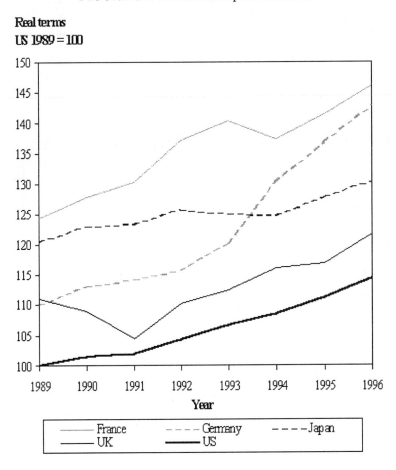

FIGURE 3.2. Evolution of price of technology

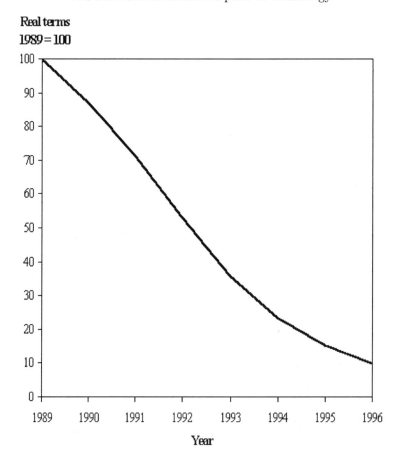

FIGURE 3.3. Evolution of mean labour/technology ratio

>20,000 empl., 1989 = 100

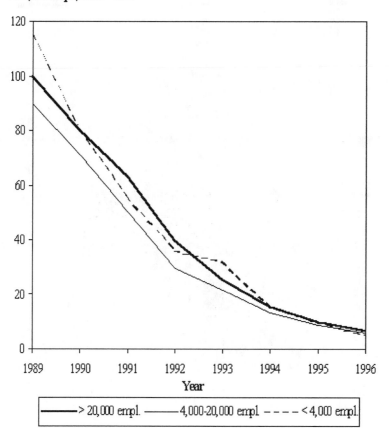

FIGURE 3.4. ξ vs. number of employees

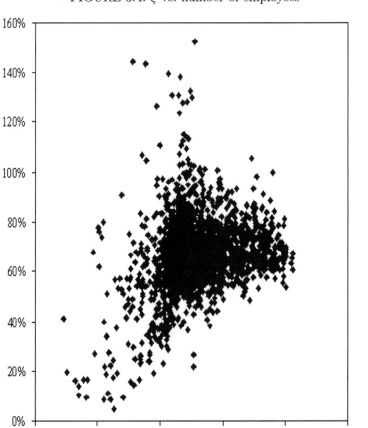

TABLE 3.1. Mean value of ξ

(1996) Country	Num. Empl. > 20,000	4,000-20,000	< 4,000
France	78.5%	76.4%	79.9%
Germany	72.0%	69.1%	64.2%
Japan	66.3%	65.6%	67.2%
UK	63.7%	67.1%	58.1%
US	67.0%	63.4%	56.3%

3.4 Empirical Specification

3.4.1 Parametric Specification

A translog approximation to the true production function was adopted in this study. With x_{it}^l and x_{it}^t representing respectively labour and technology, $f(\mathbf{x}_{it})$ was therefore approximated by (subscripts dropped):

$$f^{tl}(\mathbf{x}) = \exp\left(\begin{array}{c} a^l \ln x^l + a^t \ln x^t \\ +a^{ll} \ln x^l \ln x^l \\ +a^{tt} \ln x^t \ln x^t + a^{lt} \ln x^l \ln x^t \end{array}\right) \quad (3.1)$$

λ_{it}^t was conventionally set to zero so that, considering (2.10) and (2.11), the equations to be estimated are (subscripts dropped):

$$\ln(y) = a + a^l \ln x^l + a^t \ln x^t + a^{ll} \ln x^l \ln x^l \quad (3.2)$$
$$+a^{tt} \ln x^t \ln x^t + a^{lt} \ln x^l \ln x^t + \theta$$

$$\ln\left(\frac{m^l}{m^t}\right) = \ln\left(\frac{x^t}{x^l}\right) + \ln\left(\frac{a^l + 2a^{ll} \ln x^l + a^{lt} \ln x^t}{a^t + 2a^{tt} \ln x^t + a^{lt} \ln x^l}\right) - \lambda^l \quad (3.3)$$

3.4.2 Stochastic Specification and Estimation Methodology

Flexible panel data structures are assumed for θ_{it} and λ_{it}^l, with general heteroscedasticity, firm effects and additive AR(1) disturbances. More specifically, θ_{it} is assumed to follow:

$$\theta_{it} = \{\text{group/time effects}\} + \theta_i + v_{it}$$
$$v_{it} = p^1.v_{i,t-1} + \overline{v}_{it}, \ |p^1| < 1$$
$$E(\theta_i) = E(\overline{v}_{it}) = E(\theta_i \overline{v}_{it}) = 0$$
$$E(\theta_i \theta_j) = E(\overline{v}_{it} \overline{v}_{js}) = 0, \ for \ i \neq j$$

where the group/time effects are captured by crossed country/year dummies.[22]

Similarly, λ_{it}^l is assumed to follow:

$$
\begin{aligned}
\lambda_{it}^l &= \{\text{group/time effects}\} + \lambda_i^l + \mu_{it}^l \\
\mu_{it}^l &= p^2 \cdot \mu_{i,t-1}^l + \overline{\mu}_{it}^l, \ |p^2| < 1 \\
E\left(\lambda_i^l\right) &= E\left(\overline{\mu}_{it}^l\right) = E\left(\lambda_i^l \overline{\mu}_{it}^l\right) = 0 \\
E\left(\lambda_i^l \lambda_j^l\right) &= E\left(\overline{\mu}_{it}^l \overline{\mu}_{js}^l\right) = 0, \ for \ i \neq j
\end{aligned}
$$

where the group/time effects are also captured by crossed country/year dummies, with:

$$
E\left(\theta_i \lambda_j^l\right) = E\left(\theta_i \overline{\mu}_{jt}^l\right) = E\left(\overline{v}_{it} \lambda_j^l\right) = E\left(\overline{v}_{it} \overline{\mu}_{jt}^l\right) = 0, \ for \ i \neq j
$$

Notice that neither an Ordinary Least Squares estimator of (3.2), nor a System Least Squares estimator of (3.2) and (3.3), can be expected to provide consistent point estimates because the residuals may well be correlated with the regressors: firm effects might themselves be correlated with the regressors, and the contemporaneous shocks might include random measurement errors on the regressors.

To use lagged values of the variables as instruments, it is necessary to first remove the autocorrelative elements of the stochastic processes by performing a Durbin transformation on (3.2) and (3.3) to obtain (subscripts dropped):

$$
\begin{aligned}
\ln(y) &= a + a^l \ln x^l + a^t \ln x^t + a^{ll} \ln x^l \ln x^l \tag{3.4} \\
&\quad + a^{tt} \ln x^t \ln x^t + a^{lt} \ln x^l \ln x^t \\
&\quad + p^1 \ln y_{|-1} - p^1 \left(\begin{array}{c} a \\ + a^l \ln x_{|-1}^l + a^t \ln x_{|-1}^t \\ + a^{ll} \ln x_{|-1}^l \ln x_{|-1}^l \\ + a^{tt} \ln x_{|-1}^t \ln x_{|-1}^t \\ + a^{lt} \ln x_{|-1}^l \ln x_{|-1}^t \end{array} \right) \\
&\quad + \left(1 - p^1\right) \theta + \overline{v}
\end{aligned}
$$

[22] It is particularly important for the group/time effects on θ_{it} to be specified flexibly because, when output is replaced by its value, these group/time effects are also those assumed for output prices.

$$\ln\left(\frac{m^l}{m^t}\right) = \ln\left(\frac{x^t}{x^l}\right) \tag{3.5}$$

$$+\ln\left(\frac{a^l + 2a^{ll}\ln x^l + a^{lt}\ln x^t}{a^t + 2a^{tt}\ln x^t + a^{lt}\ln x^l}\right)$$

$$+p^2\ln\left(\frac{m^l_{|-1}}{m^t_{|-1}}\right)$$

$$-p^2\left[\begin{array}{c} \ln\left(\frac{x^t_{|-1}}{x^l_{|-1}}\right) \\ +\ln\left(\frac{a^l+2a^{ll}\ln x^l_{|-1}+a^{lt}\ln x^t_{|-1}}{a^t+2a^{tt}\ln x^t_{|-1}+a^{lt}\ln x^l_{|-1}}\right) \end{array}\right]$$

$$-\left(1-p^2\right)\lambda^l - \overline{\mu}^l$$

where $_{|-1}$ refers to once lagged variables.

Now, following Arellano and Bover (1995), assume that changes in the independent variables are not correlated with firm effects, so that differences of the independent and dependent variables lagged one or more times can be used as instruments in (3.4) and (3.5) to establish one-step and two-step (efficient) Generalised Method of Moments (GMM) estimators.

The proposed preferred estimator will be a non-linear two-step GMM estimator of (3.4) and (3.5) using once and twice lagged differences of the variables as instruments. For exploratory and comparative purposes, the following estimators will also be computed:

- linear Ordinary Least Squares on (3.4), first without imposing the common factor restrictions, and then imposing them by minimum distance;

- linear 2-Stage Least Squares (2SLS) on (3.4), using once and all available prior lagged first differences of the variables as instruments, first without imposing the common factor restrictions, and then imposing them by minimum distance;

- non-linear Seemingly Unrelated Regression Equations (SURE) on (3.4) and (3.5), which would be asymptotically equivalent to the most efficient linear estimator under the assumptions of no firm effects, no measurement error, and homoscedasticity;

- non-linear 3-Stage Least Squares (3SLS) on (3.4) and (3.5), using once and twice lagged differences of the variables as instruments, which would be efficient in the class of estimators using these instruments (and therefore equivalent to the two-step GMM estimator) under homoscedasticity.

3.4.3 Dual Characterisation

Turning to the estimation of the factor demand and actual cost derivatives as in Section 2.3.3, the chain rule needs to be repeatedly applied to (3.2) and (3.3).

More specifically, define:[23]

$$g^l \equiv a^l + 2a^{ll} \ln x^l + a^{lt} \ln x^t$$

$$g^t \equiv a^t + 2a^{tt} \ln x^t + a^{lt} \ln x^l$$

$$r \equiv \theta - \ln y$$

$$s \equiv \ln m^t - \ln m^l - \lambda^l$$

$$d \equiv 2a^{ll}\left(g^t\right)^2 - 2a^{lt}g^lg^t + 2a^{tt}\left(g^l\right)^2 - \left(g^l\right)^2 g^t - \left(g^t\right)^2 g^l$$

With these notations, and if $\langle . \rangle_i$, $\langle . \rangle_{ij}$ and $\langle . \rangle_{ijk}$ respectively represent first-order, second-order and third-order differentiation with respect to the variables i, j and k chosen in the set $\{\ln m^l, \ln m^t, \ln y, \theta, \lambda^l\}$, algebraic manipulation shows that the first-order derivatives of the demand vector can be written:

$$\left\langle \ln x^t \right\rangle_i = \frac{\langle s \rangle_i \left(g^l\right)^2 g^t + \langle r \rangle_i \left(-2a^{ll}g^t + a^{lt}g^l + g^lg^t\right)}{2a^{ll}\left(g^t\right)^2 - 2a^{lt}g^lg^t + 2a^{tt}\left(g^l\right)^2 - \left(g^l\right)^2 g^t - \left(g^t\right)^2 g^l}$$

$$\left\langle \ln x^l \right\rangle_i = -\frac{\langle r \rangle_i}{g^l} - \frac{g^t}{g^l}\left\langle \ln x^t \right\rangle_i$$

These first-order derivatives can themselves be differentiated once to obtain the second-order derivatives:

$$\left\langle \ln x^t \right\rangle_{ij} = \langle s \rangle_i \frac{2g^lg^t \left\langle g^l \right\rangle_j + \left(g^l\right)^2 \left\langle g^t \right\rangle_j}{d}$$

---

[23] Subscripts are dropped throughout this Section.

$$+ \langle r \rangle_i \frac{-2a^{ll} \langle g^t \rangle_j + a^{lt} \langle g^l \rangle_j + g^l \langle g^t \rangle_j + g^t \langle g^l \rangle_j}{d}$$

$$- \langle \ln x^t \rangle_i \frac{\langle d \rangle_j}{d}$$

$$\langle \ln x^l \rangle_{ij} = \langle r \rangle_i \frac{\langle g^l \rangle_j}{(g^l)^2} - \langle \ln x^t \rangle_i \frac{\langle g^t \rangle_j g^l - \langle g^l \rangle_j g^t}{(g^l)^2} - \langle \ln x^t \rangle_{ij} \frac{g^t}{g^l}$$

and twice to obtain the third-order derivatives:

$$\langle \ln x^t \rangle_{ijk} = \langle s \rangle_i \frac{\begin{bmatrix} 2 \langle g^l \rangle_k g^t \langle g^l \rangle_j \\ +2g^l \left(\langle g^t \rangle_k \langle g^l \rangle_j + g^t \langle g^l \rangle_{jk} \right) \\ + \left(g^l \right)^2 \langle g^t \rangle_{jk} + 2g^l \langle g^l \rangle_k \langle g^t \rangle_j \end{bmatrix}}{d}$$

$$- \langle s \rangle_i \langle d \rangle_k \frac{2g^l g^t \langle g^l \rangle_j + \left(g^l \right)^2 \langle g^t \rangle_j}{d^2}$$

$$+ \langle r \rangle_i \frac{\begin{pmatrix} -2a^{ll} \langle g^t \rangle_{jk} + a^{lt} \langle g^l \rangle_{jk} \\ + \langle g^l \rangle_k \langle g^t \rangle_j + g^l \langle g^t \rangle_{jk} \\ + \langle g^t \rangle_k \langle g^l \rangle_j + g^t \langle g^l \rangle_{jk} \end{pmatrix}}{d}$$

$$- \langle r \rangle_i \langle d \rangle_k \frac{\begin{pmatrix} -2a^{ll} \langle g^t \rangle_j + a^{lt} \langle g^l \rangle_j \\ +g^l \langle g^t \rangle_j + g^t \langle g^l \rangle_j \end{pmatrix}}{d^2}$$

$$- \langle \ln x^t \rangle_{ik} \frac{\langle d \rangle_j}{d}$$

$$- \langle \ln x^t \rangle_i \frac{\langle d \rangle_{jk} d - \langle d \rangle_j \langle d \rangle_k}{d^2}$$

$$\langle \ln x^l \rangle_{ijk} = \langle r \rangle_i \frac{\langle g^l \rangle_{jk} \left(g^l \right)^2 - 2g^l \langle g^l \rangle_k \langle g^l \rangle_j}{(g^l)^4}$$

$$- \langle \ln x^t \rangle_{ik} \frac{\langle g^t \rangle_j g^l - \langle g^l \rangle_j g^t}{(g^l)^2}$$

$$-\left\langle \ln x^t \right\rangle_i \frac{\left(\begin{array}{c} \left\langle g^t \right\rangle_{jk} g^l + \left\langle g^t \right\rangle_j \left\langle g^l \right\rangle_k \\ -\left\langle g^l \right\rangle_{jk} g^t - \left\langle g^l \right\rangle_j \left\langle g^t \right\rangle_k \end{array} \right)}{(g^l)^2}$$

$$+\left\langle \ln x^t \right\rangle_i \frac{2\left\langle g^l \right\rangle_k g^l \left(\left\langle g^t \right\rangle_j g^l + \left\langle g^l \right\rangle_j g^t \right)}{(g^l)^4}$$

$$-\left\langle \ln x^t \right\rangle_{ijk} \frac{g^t}{g^l} - \left\langle \ln x^t \right\rangle_{ij} \frac{\left\langle g^t \right\rangle_k g^l - g^t \left\langle g^l \right\rangle_k}{(g^l)^2}$$

and more generally n times to obtain the (n+1)-th order derivatives of the factor demand vector.

Similarly, applying the chain rule to (2.20) yields the first-order derivatives of ξ, the cost/income ratio:

$$\langle \xi \rangle_i = \frac{1}{y} \left(\begin{array}{c} \left\langle m^l \right\rangle_i x^l + m^l x^l \left\langle \ln x^l \right\rangle_i \\ +\left\langle m^t \right\rangle_i x^t + m^t x^t \left\langle \ln x^t \right\rangle_i \end{array} \right) \\ -\xi \left\langle \ln y \right\rangle_i$$

which can themselves be once differentiated to obtain the second-order derivatives:

$$\langle \xi \rangle_{ij} = \frac{1}{y} \left(\begin{array}{c} \left\langle m^l \right\rangle_i x^l \left\langle \ln x^l \right\rangle_j + m^l x^l \left\langle \ln x^l \right\rangle_{ij} \\ +\left\langle m^l \right\rangle_j x^l \left\langle \ln x^l \right\rangle_i + m^l x^l \left\langle \ln x^l \right\rangle_i \left\langle \ln x^l \right\rangle_j \\ +\left\langle m^t \right\rangle_i x^t \left\langle \ln x^t \right\rangle_j + m^t x^t \left\langle \ln x^t \right\rangle_{ij} \\ +\left\langle m^t \right\rangle_j x^t \left\langle \ln x^t \right\rangle_i + m^t x^t \left\langle \ln x^t \right\rangle_i \left\langle \ln x^t \right\rangle_j \end{array} \right) \\ -\xi \left\langle \ln y \right\rangle_i \left\langle \ln y \right\rangle_j - \left\langle \ln y \right\rangle_j \langle \xi \rangle_i - \left\langle \ln y \right\rangle_i \langle \xi \rangle_j$$

and twice differentiated to estimate the third-order derivatives:

$$\langle \xi \rangle_{ijk} = \langle \xi \rangle_k \frac{\langle \xi \rangle_{ij}}{\xi}$$

$$-(\xi \left\langle \ln y \right\rangle_k + \langle \xi \rangle_k) \cdot \left(\begin{array}{c} \frac{\langle \xi \rangle_{ij}}{\xi} - \frac{\langle \xi \rangle_j \langle \xi \rangle_i}{\xi^2} \\ + \left[\begin{array}{c} \left(\left\langle \ln y \right\rangle_j + \frac{\langle \xi \rangle_j}{\xi} \right) * \\ \left(\left\langle \ln y \right\rangle_i + \frac{\langle \xi \rangle_i}{\xi} \right) \end{array} \right] \end{array} \right)$$

$$
+\frac{1}{y}
\begin{bmatrix}
\left\langle m^l \right\rangle_i x^l \left\langle \ln x^l \right\rangle_k \left\langle \ln x^l \right\rangle_j + \left\langle m^l \right\rangle_i x^l \left\langle \ln x^l \right\rangle_{jk} \\
+ \left\langle m^l \right\rangle_k x^l \left\langle \ln x^l \right\rangle_{ij} \\
+ m^l \begin{pmatrix} x^l \left\langle \ln x^l \right\rangle_k \left\langle \ln x^l \right\rangle_{ij} \\ + x^l \left\langle \ln x^l \right\rangle_{ijk} \end{pmatrix} \\
+ \left\langle m^l \right\rangle_j x^l \left\langle \ln x^l \right\rangle_k \left\langle \ln x^l \right\rangle_i + \left\langle m^l \right\rangle_j x^l \left\langle \ln x^l \right\rangle_{ik} \\
+ \left\langle m^l \right\rangle_k x^l \left\langle \ln x^l \right\rangle_i \left\langle \ln x^l \right\rangle_j \\
+ m^l \begin{pmatrix} x^l \left\langle \ln x^l \right\rangle_i \left\langle \ln x^l \right\rangle_j \left\langle \ln x^l \right\rangle_k \\ + x^l \left\langle \ln x^l \right\rangle_{ik} \left\langle \ln x^l \right\rangle_j \\ + x^l \left\langle \ln x^l \right\rangle_i \left\langle \ln x^l \right\rangle_{jk} \end{pmatrix} \\
+ \left\langle m^t \right\rangle_i x^t \left\langle \ln x^t \right\rangle_k \left\langle \ln x^t \right\rangle_j + \left\langle m^t \right\rangle_i x^t \left\langle \ln x^t \right\rangle_{jk} \\
+ \left\langle m^t \right\rangle_k x^t \left\langle \ln x^t \right\rangle_{ij} \\
+ m^t \begin{pmatrix} x^t \left\langle \ln x^t \right\rangle_k \left\langle \ln x^t \right\rangle_{ij} \\ + x^t \left\langle \ln x^t \right\rangle_{ijk} \end{pmatrix} \\
+ \left\langle m^t \right\rangle_j x^t \left\langle \ln x^t \right\rangle_k \left\langle \ln x^t \right\rangle_i + \left\langle m^t \right\rangle_j x^t \left\langle \ln x^t \right\rangle_{ik} \\
+ \left\langle m^t \right\rangle_k x^t \left\langle \ln x^t \right\rangle_i \left\langle \ln x^t \right\rangle_j \\
+ m^t \begin{pmatrix} x^t \left\langle \ln x^t \right\rangle_i \left\langle \ln x^t \right\rangle_j \left\langle \ln x^t \right\rangle_k \\ + x^t \left\langle \ln x^t \right\rangle_{ik} \left\langle \ln x^t \right\rangle_j \\ + x^t \left\langle \ln x^t \right\rangle_i \left\langle \ln x^t \right\rangle_{jk} \end{pmatrix}
\end{bmatrix}
$$

$$
- \left(\left\langle \xi \right\rangle_{ik} - \frac{\left\langle \xi \right\rangle_i \left\langle \xi \right\rangle_k}{\xi} \right) \left\langle \ln y \right\rangle_j
$$

$$
- \left(\left\langle \xi \right\rangle_{jk} - \frac{\left\langle \xi \right\rangle_j \left\langle \xi \right\rangle_k}{\xi} \right) \left\langle \ln y \right\rangle_i
$$

and in general differentiated n times to obtain the (n+1)-th order derivatives of the cost/income ratio.

4
Empirical Results

This Chapter summarises the main empirical findings of the current study, with a particular emphasis on the issues raised in Section 3.1. More precisely, Section 4.1 presents the econometric estimation results and the statistical evidence as to the optimising behaviour of firms. Section 4.2 examines scale effects from both a primal and a dual perspective. Section 4.3 seeks to identify the extent and cost consequences of sub-optimal capacity utilisation in general, and of disequilibrium induced by labour market rigidities in particular. Finally, Section 4.4 presents a breakdown of the 1996 differences in international cost/income ratios into price, scale, technical efficiency and capacity utilisation effects.

4.1   Econometric Results

4.1.1   Single Equation Estimation: Core Results

Tables 4.1 and 4.2 present the results of least squares and instrumental variables estimation of (3.4) using the DPD97 unbalanced panel data program of M. Arellano and S. Bond.[1]

The results reported in Tables 4.1 and 4.2 seem generally consistent with the assumed stochastic specification and point to the superiority of the instrumental variables estimator (TL3), which provides some evidence of persistent (firm effect induced) positive correlation in the residuals and allows the imposition of the implied common factor restrictions that yield (TL4).[2]

---

[1] In fact, all the single equation estimators presented in Section 4.1 were computed by DPD97 which was kindly made available, along with many hours of invaluable tutoring, by Steve Bond.

[2] Compare the p-value on the common factor restrictions test for (TL1) and (TL3). This test was not conducted on a two-step GMM estimator as Arellano and Bond (1991) provide simulation results indicating that the estimated covariance matrix of two-step GMM estimators may be biased downward in finite samples.

TABLE 4.1. Production function estimation: results

	(TL1)	(TL2)	(TL3)	(TL4)
Tech.	**OLS**	**OLS**	**2SLS**	**2SLS**
Com. fac. rest.	not imposed	imposed	not imposed	imposed
a^l	-0.5146	-0.3300	-0.9596	-0.6692
	(0.5230)	(0.1629)	(1.6490)	(0.2422)
a^t	0.4846	0.5359	0.1086	0.4267
	(0.1013)	(0.0636)	(0.4445)	(0.1034)
a^{ll}	0.0956	0.0938	0.0746	0.0849
	(0.0301)	(0.0108)	(0.0715)	(0.0167)
a^{tt}	0.0297	0.0428	-0.0032	0.0297
	(0.0075)	(0.0046)	(0.0329)	(0.0093)
a^{lt}	-0.0707	-0.0955	0.0443	-0.0412
	(0.0169)	(0.0105)	(0.1055)	(0.0252)
pl	0.6762	0.7992	0.4395	0.5398
	(0.1003)	(0.0238)	(0.1757)	(0.0266)
$a^l * p^l$	-0.3643	--	-0.4472	--
	(0.4754)		(1.3898)	
$a^t * p^l$	0.2191	--	-0.3795	--
	(0.1371)		(0.6608)	
$a^{ll} * p^l$	0.0616	--	0.0032	--
	(0.0215)		(0.0551)	
$a^{tt} * p^l$	0.0081	--	-0.0375	--
	(0.0131)		(0.0457)	
$a^{lt} * p^l$	-0.0259	--	0.1200	--
	(0.0281)		(0.1388)	
1st-order corr.	-1.310	--	2.360	--
	(0.190)		(0.018)	
2nd-order corr.	1.211	--	1.800	--
	(0.226)		(0.072)	
Com. fac. rest.	15.445	--	3.756	--
	(0.009)		(0.585)	
Cobb-Douglas	75.385	--	25.096	--
	(0.000)		(0.000)	

TABLE 4.2. Production function estimation: notes

Dataset is unbalanced panel on 482 G-5 banks
in the period 1989-1996, with a total of
2,322 observations.
Crossed country/year dummies included in
production function.
Entries in parentheses are robust estimates of
asymptotic standard errors for point estimates
and p-values for test statistics.
(TL1) & (TL3): Serial correlation tests are
distributed standard normal; common factor and
Cobb-Douglas tests are distributed chi-squared.
(TL2) & (TL4): Common factor restrictions
imposed on unrestricted autoregressive distributed
lag estimates by minimum distance.
(TL3) & (TL4): Instruments are dummies as well
as once and prior lagged first diff. of the variables.
(TL3): Sargan test of overidentifying restrictions,
based on unrestricted GMM 2-step estimator,
is 128.673 (p-value: 0.181).

4.1.2 Single Equation Estimation: Restrictions and Extensions

Although Cobb-Douglas restrictions can clearly not be justified on the basis of the evidence presented in Tables 4.1 and 4.2, the results of single equation estimation of (3.4) under a Cobb-Douglas specification are reported in Table 4.3 for comparative purposes.

While the results in Table 4.3 are generally consistent with those in Tables 4.1 and 4.2, comparing the point estimates in (CD2) and (CD4) suggests the presence of a phenomenon obscured in Table 4.1 by the complexity of the functional form: significant measurement error on technology.[3]

Additionally, the validity of the point estimates in (TL4) for banks of different sizes was tested by examining two extensions to the chosen parametric specification.

Firstly, third-order terms were added to (3.4): while the results obtained were consistent with those reported in Tables 4.1 and 4.3, the Wald test of significance of the third-order terms allowed their rejection at the 5% level (p-value: 0.145).

Secondly, the sample was split into two sub-samples, one consisting of small banks, and one consisting of medium-sized and large banks: the single equation estimators of (3.4) were computed separately for each sub-sample, but the econometric results did not indicate statistically significant differences in the point estimates.[4]

The point estimates in (TL4) therefore seem to be valid for both smaller and larger banks.

---

[3] Interestingly, the evolution of the coefficients in (CD2) and (CD4) is quite similar to that found by Olley and Pakes (1996) in their estimation of a Cobb-Douglas production function for the telecommunications industry: relatively little change in the coefficient on labour and a doubling of the coefficient on capital when one compares the least squares and the consistent estimators. Many other studies have documented the tendency to obtain implausibly low capital productivity estimates because of measurement issues; see for instance Griliches and Mairesse (1983;1990), Mairesse and Kremp (1993), and Hall and Mairesse (1995).

[4] More specifically, the point estimates all lay well within each other's confidence intervals, with higher standard errors for the sub-sample estimators than for the estimator on the entire sample.

TABLE 4.3. Cobb-Douglas estimation

	(CD1)	(CD2)	(CD3)	(CD4)
Tech.	**OLS**	**OLS**	**2SLS**	**2SLS**
Com. fac. rest.	not imposed	imposed	not imposed	imposed
a^l	0.5649	0.5826	0.4964	0.4023
	(0.0661)	(0.2054)	(0.1771)	(0.1490)
a^i	0.2582	0.2054	0.5144	0.5550
	(0.0368)	(0.0249)	(0.1760)	(0.1046)
$p\,l$	0.7490	0.967	0.3984	0.5409
	(0.0842)	(0.0336)	(0.1826)	(0.1225)
$a^l *p^l$	0.4672	--	0.3592	--
	(0.0918)		(0.1896)	
$a^i *p^l$	0.1251	--	0.1256	--
	(0.0235)		(0.1003)	
1st-order corr.	-1.319	--	2.597	--
	(0.187)		(0.009)	
2nd-order corr.	1.231	--	2.200	--
	(0.218)		(0.028)	
Com. fac. rest.	18.925	--	2.939	--
	(0.000)		(0.230)	

Notes

Dataset is unbalanced panel on 482 G-5 banks in the period 1989-1996, with a total of 2,322 observations.

Crossed country/year dummies included in production function.

Entries in parentheses are robust estimates of asymptotic standard errors for point estimates and p-values for test statistics.

(CD1) & (CD3): Serial correlation tests are distributed standard normal; common factor tests are distributed chi-squared.

(CD2) & (CD4): Common factor restrictions imposed on unrestricted autoregressive distributed lag estimates by minimum distance.

(CD3) & (CD4): Instruments are dummies as well as once and prior lagged first diff. of the variables.

(CD3): Sargan test of overidentifying restrictions, based on unrestricted GMM 2-step estimator, is 49.632 (p-value: 0.775).

4.1.3   System Estimation

The results of non-linear estimation of (3.4) and (3.5) are presented in Table 4.4, including those relating to the two-step GMM estimator using once and twice lagged differences of the variables.

Notice that the evolution of the standard error estimates from (TL4) to (TL7) is consistent with a gain in efficiency.[5] Also, the test statistics in (TL7) indicate an unambiguous rejection of:

- the neo-classical restriction, under which λ_{it} is supposed to be zero everywhere;[6]

- the "Toda" restriction,[7] assumed explicitly or implicitly in most previous shadow cost based empirical work, which literally implies that λ_{it} is fixed for all sampled observations but which was taken in this multi-national context to signify that λ_{it} is the same for observations stemming from the same country.

Since no statistical evidence seems to support either neo-classical or previous shadow cost models, FCM can be considered, at least in the current context, a genuine improvement over these two classes of models.

The point estimates in (TL7) were used to derive the empirical results reported in the following Sections.[8]

---

[5]However, as previously discussed, the estimated standard errors of the two-step GMM estimator may well be biased downward.

[6]The test for the neo-classical hypothesis, like the one for the "Toda" hypothesis discussed further, was constructed by considering the restrictions implied by the null hypothesis on the coefficients relating to the crossed country/year dummy variables in (3.5).

[7]Referring to Toda (1976).

[8]As shown in the second table presented in the Appendix, the production function regularity conditions are met for 96% of all observations, and for no less than 67% of the observations in any of the country/size/year sub-samples.

TABLE 4.4. System estimation

Tech.	(TL5) NL SURE	(TL6) NL 3SLS	(TL7) NL 2-STEP GMM
Com. fac. rest.	imposed	imposed	imposed
a^l	-0.6811	-0.5817	-0.7285
	(0.5972)	(0.0734)	(0.0998)
a^t	0.3905	0.1859	0.3311
	(0.2888)	(0.0873)	(0.1003)
a^{ll}	0.0899	0.0685	0.0931
	(0.0770)	(0.0114)	(0.0154)
a^{tt}	0.0361	0.0421	0.0409
	(0.0146)	(0.0048)	(0.0037)
a^{lt}	-0.0499	-0.0278	-0.0554
	(0.0395)	(0.0148)	(0.0164)
p^l	0.7884	0.4117	0.7680
	(0.4437)	(0.1712)	(0.0796)
p^t	0.8197	0.9437	0.9919
	(0.0239)	(0.0246)	(0.0309)
Cobb-Douglas	6.180 (0.103)	566.078 (0.000)	1105.085 (0.000)
Neo-Classical	13.852 (0.999)	311.382 (0.000)	491.850 (0.000)
Toda*	10.731 (1.000)	64.596 (0.000)	83.070 (0.000)

Notes

Joint estimation of production function and first-order condition. Dataset is unbalanced panel on 514 G-5 banks in the period 1989-1996, with a total of 2315 observations. Crossed Country/Year dummies included in production function and first-order condition. Entries in parentheses are robust estimates of asymptotic standard errors for point estimates and p-values for test statistics. (TL6) & (TL7): Instruments are dummies as well as once and twice lagged first differences of the variables. (TL6): Sargan test of overidentifying restrictions is 107.935 (p-value: 0.000). (TL7): Sargan test of overidentifying restrictions is 24.213 (p-value: 0.114).

*i.e., same allocative efficiency index for observations stemming from same country.

4.1.4 Evidence of Output Measurement Error

Since output was replaced in this study by its value (converted to 1996 US dollars), the production function residuals can be expected to include output price noise and their evolution over time should reflect the influence of two opposing factors:

- the technical efficiency indices θ_{it} which in all likelihood follow an upward trend;

- an output price noise which, because of the decrease in the general level of bank prices during the period 1989-1996, presumably follows a downward trend.

As it turns out, and as is illustrated in Figure 4.1 for large banks, the measured production function residuals actually slope downward, therefore pointing to significant output price noise.

Production function residuals must therefore be interpreted with extreme care, especially in a time series context where they clearly cannot be assumed to represent proper proxies for the θ_{it} process.

4.2 Scale Effects

Before discussing empirical results as to the existence and extent of scale effects, a word of caution is needed with respect to a fundamental identification issue between scale effects and technical efficiency, when technical efficiency is defined as in equation (2.5) — i.e., as the observation-specific deviation between the dependent variable and a function of the independent variables.

This identification issue stems from the concurrence of two elements:

- the high dependence on parametric specification of empirical measurements of scale effects and technical efficiency: generally, the more flexible the functional form chosen for empirical purposes, the better the fit and the more variations in the dependent variable will be attributed to scale effects rather than to differences in degrees of technical efficiency;[9]

---

[9]Taking matters to the extreme, if the number of free parameters in the chosen functional form is close to the number of observations, the fit will be close to perfect

FIGURE 4.1. Evolution of mean production function residual

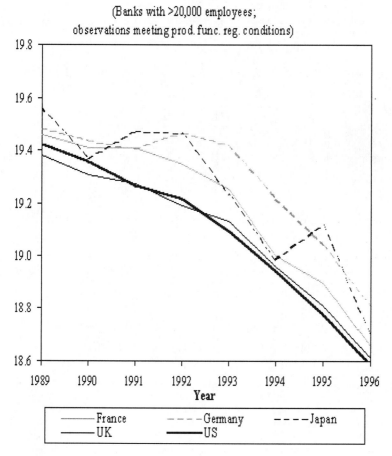

(Banks with >20,000 employees;
observations meeting prod. func. reg. conditions)

- the fact that, although heuristics can help choose an appropriate functional form,[10] this choice is to some extent discretionary.

Therefore, in a very fundamental sense, and although this issue seems somewhat ignored in the empirical literature, measuring scale effects and technical efficiency is contingent on the chosen parametric form — i.e., in the present context, on the assumption that the proper functional form is a second-order translog.

4.2.1 Primal Measurement

The pattern of scale effects can be most directly studied through the usual production-side metric:

$$\kappa_{it} = \frac{\partial \ln f\,(k\mathbf{x}_{it})}{\partial \ln k}\Big|_{k=1}$$

which, considering (3.2), simplifies to:

$$\kappa_{it} = a^l + a^t + \left(2a^{ll} + a^{lt}\right)\ln x_{it}^l + \left(2a^{tt} + a^{lt}\right)\ln x_{it}^t$$

This primal metric was computed for all observations, and is plotted in Figure 4.2 against bank size.

Scale diseconomies (i.e., $\kappa_{it} < 1$) seem to exist for small banks,[11] and increasing scale economies for banks with more than $\sim$10,000 employees,[12] so that the implied average cost curve assumes an inverted U-shape.

This pattern was discussed with several experts on banking technology who suggested the following rationale.[13] As banks evolve

---

and virtually no variations in the dependent variable would be attributed to efficiency differences.

[10] For instance, if the proper functional approximation is assumed to be translog, higher-order terms can readily be added or subtracted on the basis of econometric evidence. This is of course the heuristic followed in Section 4.1.2 — a heuristic which suggested that a second-order translog was "optimal" as second-order terms were statistically significant while third-order ones were not.

[11] For very small banks, this seems consistent with Berger et al. (1987) who found significant diseconomies of scale for US single office unit banks.

[12] The extent of scale economies in Figure 4.2 for banks with more than $\sim$10,000 employees seems consistent with the findings of Evanoff et al. (1990) who reported for the 164 largest US banks an average cost-side scale metric of $\sim$0.92 (i.e., corresponding to a primal metric of $\sim$1.09).

[13] The remarks of Elias Baltassis and John Pries, from the Mitchell Madison Group, were particularly insightful.

FIGURE 4.2. κ vs. number of employees

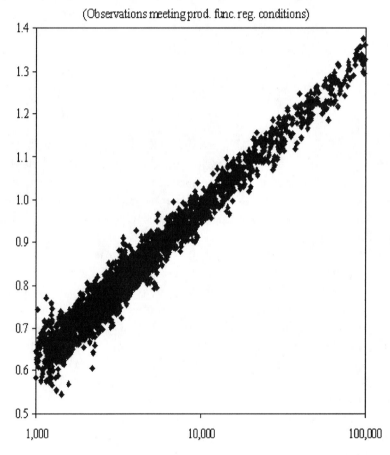

(Observations meeting prod. func. reg. conditions)

over the size spectrum, their technology requirements dramatically change. Small banks typically purchase external business-specific software, offer a limited set of standard products and run product, accounting and customer management applications on inexpensive PC- and workstation-based local area networks (LANs). As banks get larger, they must cope with increasing processing volumes and product proliferation; they rapidly exhaust the technical capabilities of off-the-shelf software and LANs and incur scale diseconomies during the costly migration towards high fixed-cost, mainframe-based architectures. Large banks, on the other hand, leverage technological infrastructures conducive to high volumes; when they expand output, they are able to reap scale economies as the high fixed cost of these infrastructures is spread over a larger revenue base.

4.2.2   Dual Measurement

Turning to a dual characterisation of scale effects, the derivations in Section 3.4.3 allow the computation of the derivatives of the cost/income ratio with respect to the logarithm of output. Figure 4.3 plots the first-order derivative of the cost/income ratio as a function of output.[14]

As expected, Figure 4.3 confirms the pattern identified in Figure 4.2; in particular, notice that, for larger banks, the derivative of the cost/income ratio with respect to output is negative and declining.

Upon closer examination, the cost/income ratio turns out to be a highly non-linear function of the logarithm of output. This is illustrated by Figure 4.4, which shows the evolution of the second-order derivative of the cost/income ratio (with respect to the logarithm of output) as a function of output and which still exhibits non-linear behaviour.[15]

Notice now in Figures 4.3 and 4.4 that if a fourth-order polynomial is fitted through the first-order derivative, and a third-order polynomial through the second-order derivative, the latter polynomial does

---

[14] In the Figures presented in this Section, observations are screened not only for the usual production function regularity conditions, but also for the capacity utilisation conditions discussed in Section 2.3.3; for details on the empirical establishment of these capacity utilisation regularity conditions, see Section 4.3.2.

[15] The third-order derivative was examined and also turned out to be a non-linear function of output. This strong non-linearity proved resistant to transformations of the variables.

FIGURE 4.3. $\frac{\partial \xi}{\partial \ln y}$ vs. logarithm of output value

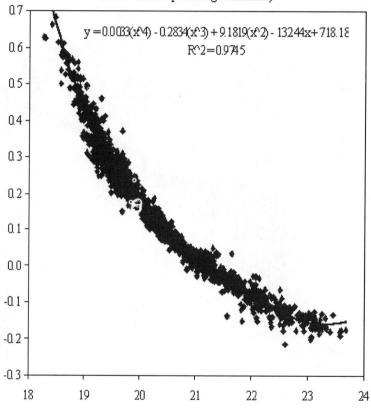

(Observations meeting prod. func.
and 3d.-order cap. util. reg. conditions)

$y = 0.0033(x^4) - 0.2834(x^3) + 9.1819(x^2) - 132.44x + 718.18$

$R^2 = 0.9745$

FIGURE 4.4. $\frac{\partial^2 \xi}{\partial \ln y \partial \ln y}$ vs. logarithm of output value

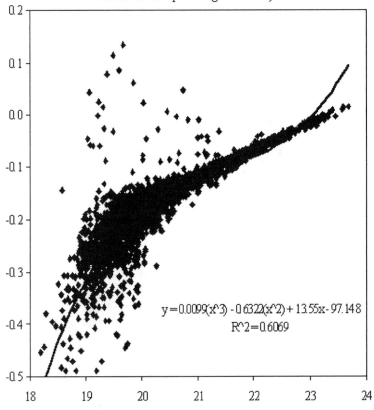

(Observations meeting prod. func.
and 3d.-order cap. util. reg. conditions)

$y = 0.0099(x^3) - 0.6322(x^2) + 13.55x - 97.148$
$R^2 = 0.6069$

seem to be approximately equivalent to the derivative of the first one.[16] In the hope that this process can be reversed with impunity, the curve in Figure 4.3 was integrated to provide an estimate of the ceteris paribus relation, in levels, between the cost/income ratio and the logarithm of output.

Figure 4.5 presents these integrated values of the cost/income ratio, as a function of bank size and normalised to zero for banks with about 2,500 employees.

As expected, the curve in Figure 4.5 assumes an inverted U-shape. The fundamental relation seems to be that, as banks evolve from ~2,500 to ~10,000 employees, their cost/income ratio increases (additively) by about 19%, and a multiplication by ten of size, from ~10,000 to ~100,000 employees, is necessary for the cost/income ratio to regain its initial level.

But, comparing Figures 4.5 and 3.4, an immediate issue arises. While in Figure 3.4 the cost/income ratio does increase until ~10,000 employees, it does not seem to decrease from ~10,000 to ~100,000 employees. What impedes the fall of the cost/income ratio for banks with more than ~10,000 employees? More precisely, what other effects compensate for the improvement in cost position that should be expected for large banks on the basis of scale effects?

One theoretically possible counteracting effect is capacity utilisation. However, as will be shown in the next Section, the capacity utilisation levels of smaller banks are in fact generally worse than those for larger banks,[17] so that capacity utilisation effects reinforce rather than mitigate the expectation of dropping cost/income ratios for banks with more than ~10,000 employees.

The solution, then, must be found in the examination of price and technical efficiency effects, and an analysis of the production function residuals confirms that they are indeed negatively correlated with size for banks with more than ~4,000 employees.

It is unfortunately impossible to determine from the available data how much of this pattern may be due to output price versus to technical efficiency effects. In all likelihood, however, output price

---

[16] This property does not hold for the third-order derivative, which turns out to be much more non-linear than would be expected by the differentiation of the third-order polynomial fitted through the second-order derivative.

[17] This explains why cost/income ratios in Figure 3.4 do not increase in the 2,500-10,000 employee range as much as expected from Figure 4.5.

FIGURE 4.5. ξ vs. number of employees: ceteris paribus relation

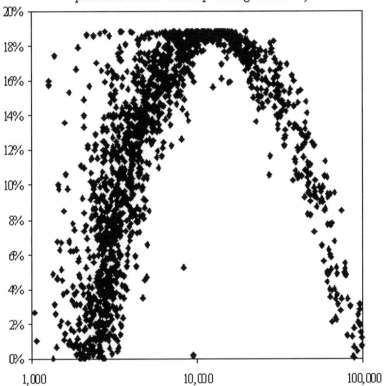

(Normalised to zero for banks
with ~2,500 employees; observations meeting
prod. func. and 3d-order cap. util. reg. conditions)

differences are to blame: the product mix generally evolves in the 4,000-100,000 employee range away from a focus on high-margin, geographically focused retail products towards a diversified product range including marginally profitable activities such as payments processing, trading and international wholesale lending.[18]

The presence of latent differences in output prices may also provide an econometric explanation as to why most previous studies found no significant scale economies for large banks. As mentioned in Section 3.2, the econometric estimation of shadow cost and neoclassical models is complicated by the presence of output measurement error: since output occurs in cost based models as an independent variable,[19] output measurement error generates correlations between some regressors and the error term. These correlations are particularly troublesome in light of the fact that previous cost function based banking studies have generally not used instrumental variables estimation and may therefore have generated inconsistent point estimates on regressors involving output.

4.3   Capacity Utilisation Effects

4.3.1   Allocative Efficiency Indices

The first-order condition residuals, which can be equated with λ_{it} even in the presence of output price noise, have generally been declining over time. This is illustrated by Figure 4.6 for large banks.

As expected, Figure 4.6 indicates that banks have increasingly suffered from excess labour. Also, in more recent years, excess labour seems to have been more significant for Continental European banks than for UK and US banks; from equation (2.11), this phenomenon has been due to two distinct causes: higher labour cost (Figure 3.1) and higher labour/technology ratio (Figure 3.3).

Upon closer examination of Figure 4.6, two more surprising facts emerge.

Firstly, large US banks actually started out in 1989 with insufficient labour. This finding is consistent with Evanoff et al. (1990)

---

[18] The largest G-5 banks tend to have about half of their assets invested outside their home country in low-margin wholesale lending.

[19] And output is invariably measured through some value proxy — usually "total assets".

FIGURE 4.6. Evolution of mean value of λ

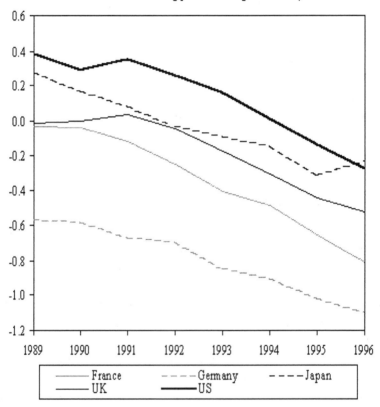

(Banks with > 20,000 employees;
observations meeting prod. func. reg. conditions)

who, using a simple shadow cost function approach (i.e., assuming a fixed λ_{it}) and a more traditional definition of capital, found an average value of the labour allocative efficiency index of ~0.58 for large US banks in the period 1972-1987. Evanoff et al. rationalised this finding by pointing to possible strategic behaviour in a regulated environment, and in particular to a so-called "commitment theory":

> "Decreased competition resulting from regulations may enable management to pursue a strategy to convince customers that the bank is a credible and viable alternative that will be in the market over the long-haul. One means to achieve this objective would be for management to spend large sums to generate an imposing physical structure."

A rationale for insufficient labour in the 1980s, which may appear more compelling in light of the subsequent evolution in Figure 4.6, is that banks anticipated early on that technology prices would keep dropping dramatically,[20] and that they would experience significant factor mix adjustment difficulties. Consequently, US banks, solving a multi-period optimisation problem, found it optimal to preemptively reduce their labour/technology ratios — an option not available to European banks facing stiff labour market rigidities.

Secondly, large Japanese banks seem to have followed an adjustment path similar to that of large US banks. This observation must however be discounted because of the minimal sample sizes involved: as indicated in the first table presented in the Appendix, the dataset includes only one large Japanese bank in 1989 and two in the period 1990-1996.

Table 4.5, which provides a breakdown of the average values of λ_{it} by bank size indicates yet another interesting pattern.

Clearly, allocative efficiency seems to be correlated with bank size, with small banks generally suffering the most from excess labour in recent years. This pattern may reflect difficulties encountered by small banks needing to engage in the considerable capital invest-

---

[20] "Moore's law", according to which the price/performance ratio of microprocessors drops by about half every 18 months, has been widely known at least since the early 1980s.

ments required for automation: they may simply *"not have the dollars to invest"*.[21]

TABLE 4.5. Mean value of λ: detail

(Observations meeting prod. func. reg. conditions)

Country	Num. Empl.	1989	1990	1991	1992	1993	1994	1995	1996
France	> 20,000	-0.03	-0.05	-0.12	-0.25	-0.40	-0.49	-0.66	-0.81
	4,000-20,000	-0.06	-0.13	-0.22	-0.31	-0.52	-0.62	-0.83	-1.03
	< 4,000	-0.14	-0.26	-0.32	-0.52	-0.72	-0.85	-1.07	-1.05
Germany	> 20,000	-0.57	-0.58	-0.67	-0.69	-0.84	-0.90	-1.02	-1.10
	4,000-20,000	-0.34	-0.41	-0.51	-0.63	-0.56	-0.60	-0.82	-0.85
	< 4,000	-0.34	-0.45	-0.55	-0.73	-0.98	-1.24	-1.38	-1.45
Japan	> 20,000	0.28	0.17	0.09	-0.03	-0.09	-0.15	-0.32	-0.23
	4,000-20,000	-0.04	-0.07	-0.12	-0.23	-0.43	-0.59	-0.75	-0.77
	< 4,000	-0.24	-0.32	-0.43	-0.56	-0.74	-0.92	-1.06	-1.10
UK	> 20,000	-0.01	0.00	0.04	-0.05	-0.18	-0.31	-0.44	-0.53
	4,000-20,000	0.00	0.04	-0.09	-0.11	-0.53	-0.65	-0.81	-0.65
	< 4,000	-0.27	-0.19	-0.28	-0.36	-0.36	-0.53	-0.76	-0.93
US	> 20,000	0.39	0.29	0.35	0.26	0.16	0.01	-0.14	-0.27
	4,000-20,000	0.19	0.26	0.25	0.19	0.03	-0.12	-0.28	-0.44
	< 4,000	0.40	0.34	0.33	0.10	-0.05	-0.20	-0.40	-0.62

At a finer level, even within given country/size/year sub-samples, significant degrees of heterogeneity exist in the individual values of λ_{it}.[22] Figure 4.7, for instance, shows the considerable dispersion in the individual values of the allocative efficiency index in the case of medium-sized US banks in 1994.

This firm-level heterogeneity validates the inclusion of firm effects in the stochastic specification in Section 3.4.2. and indicates that there is no empirical basis for the assumption that allocative efficiency residuals are any less dispersed than technical efficiency residuals.

---

[21] Charles Wendel, *American Banker*, March 30, 1998.

[22] Within sub-samples, differences in allocative efficiency could be due to many bank-specific factors. For example, firms enjoying high (internal) growth rates should be relatively more able to dynamically adjust their factor mix — under the assumption that employment is easier to increase than to decrease. Also, firms with age pyramids skewed towards older employees might find it easier to shed labour through scheduled or accelerated retirements.

FIGURE 4.7. Distribution of λ

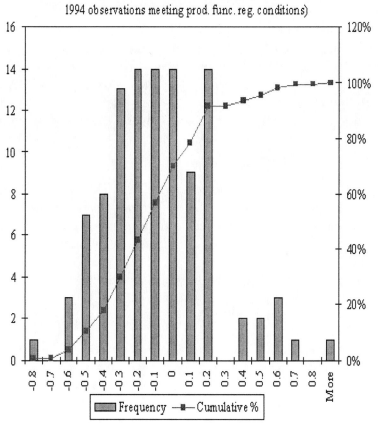

(US banks with 4,000-20,000 employees;
1994 observations meeting prod. func. reg. conditions)

Considering further the allocative and technical efficiency residuals, Figure 4.8 plots the production function residuals as a function of the allocative efficiency indices and indicates that banks with the highest λ_{it} values appear to be those with the best technical efficiency residuals.

But Figure 4.8 is polluted by output price noise and, under the assumption that banks in the same country/size/year sub-sample face similar output prices, this noise can be filtered out by limiting the analysis to banks in the same sub-sample. Figures 4.9 and 4.10 present the results for two sub-samples of reasonable density: US medium-sized and small banks in 1994.

Interestingly, Figures 4.9 and 4.10 point to a U-shaped relation between technical and allocative efficiency indices. Banks with the worse factor mixes, either because they have too much or not enough labour, seem to attempt to compensate for this competitive handicap by being particularly efficient in a technical sense.[23]

4.3.2   Capacity Utilisation Rates

With estimates of the λ_{it} indices and of the factor demand derivatives with respect to λ_{it} (from the derivations in Section 3.4.3), Taylor expansions allow the estimation of the input-specific capacity utilisation rates φ_{it}^l and φ_{it}^t by approximating the impact on factor demand of driving λ_{it} to zero.

As discussed in Section 2.3.4, a key issue here is: to what degree should the Taylor expansion be carried out? Three consistency criteria were proposed in Section 2.3.4:

- two capacity utilisation regularity conditions: the estimated input levels should be strictly positive and estimated minimum cost should be lower than (presumably sub-optimal) current cost;

---

[23] Also, remark in Figures 4.9 and 4.10 that fitted second-order polynomials do seem to reach their minimum value when λ_{it} is approximately zero, indicating that banks which enjoy optimal factor mixes tend to be the least technically efficient ones.

FIGURE 4.8. Production function residual vs. λ

(Observations meeting prod. func. reg. conditions)

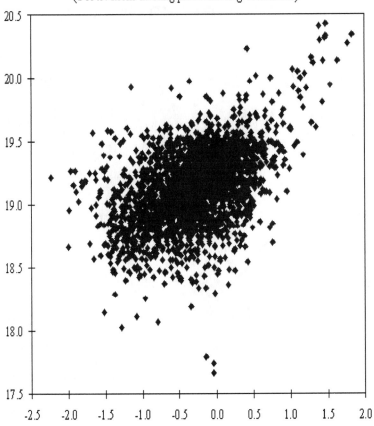

FIGURE 4.9. Production function residual vs. λ: first sub-sample

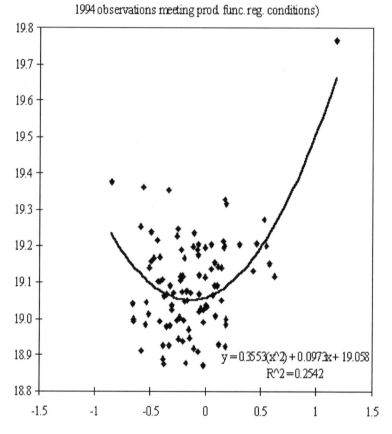

(US banks with 4,000-20,000 employees;
1994 observations meeting prod. func. reg. conditions)

$y = 0.3553(x^2) + 0.0973x + 19.058$
$R^2 = 0.2542$

FIGURE 4.10. Production function residual vs. λ: second sub-sample

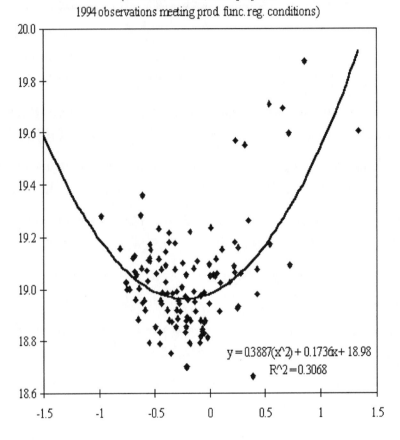

(US banks with < 4,000 employees;
1994 observations meeting prod. func. reg. conditions)

$$y = 0.3887(x^2) + 0.1736x + 18.98$$
$$R^2 = 0.3068$$

- a distributional property: if the estimated optimum factor input levels are injected back into the production function, the computed value of output should be close to its actual value so that, for proper approximations, the distribution of the output approximation error should be clustered around zero.[24]

Consider first the distribution of the output approximation error for observations meeting the required regularity conditions. Figure 4.11 shows this distribution for first-order Taylor approximations of the optimum levels of labour and technology.

Clearly, the distribution in Figure 4.11 is not satisfactory: it is skewed towards negative values and therefore indicates that firms could in fact not reproduce their current output levels with the approximated input levels.

Moving on to higher-order expansions, Figure 4.12 shows the same distribution for second-order Taylor series estimations of the optimum input levels.

Notice that the pattern in Figure 4.12 presents a significant improvement over the one in Figure 4.11, with the output approximation error properly clustered around zero.

Finally, turning to third-order Taylor expansions, the corresponding distribution of output approximation errors is shown in Figure 4.13.

On the one hand, a comparison of Figures 4.12 and 4.13 suggests that third-order expansions may be more accurate than second-order ones. On the other hand, an examination of the underlying estimated input values indicates mostly insignificant differences, therefore suggesting that it may not be necessary to carry the Taylor expansions any further.

Upon closer analysis of the outliers in Figures 4.12 and 4.13, it appears that neither the second- nor the third-order expansions are in fact sufficiently reliable for some of the observations with highly negative initial values of the allocative efficiency index. Consider indeed Table 4.6 which reports the third-order mean output approximation error for each country/size/year sub-sample.

---

[24] As mentioned in Section 2.3.4., this line of reasoning is in fact contingent on the assumption that the estimated production function provides an adequate approximation to the true production function in the neighbourhood of the optimised levels of factor inputs.

FIGURE 4.11. Output approximation error: first-order Taylor series

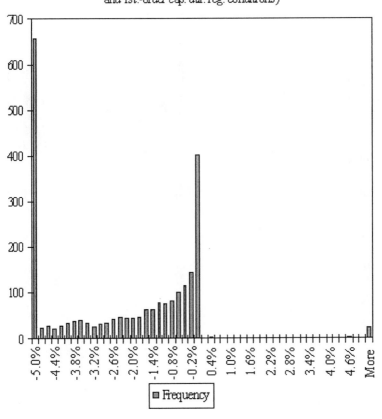

(Observations meeting prod. func.
and 1st.-order cap. util. reg. conditions)

FIGURE 4.12. Output approximation error: second-order Taylor series

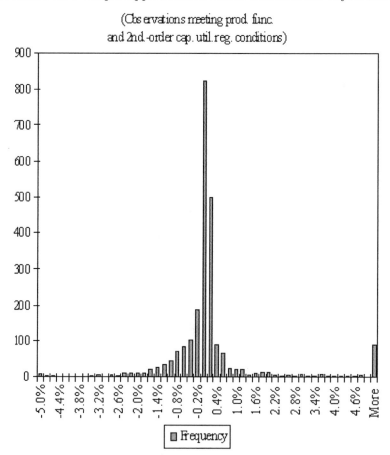

FIGURE 4.13. Output approximation error: third-order Taylor series

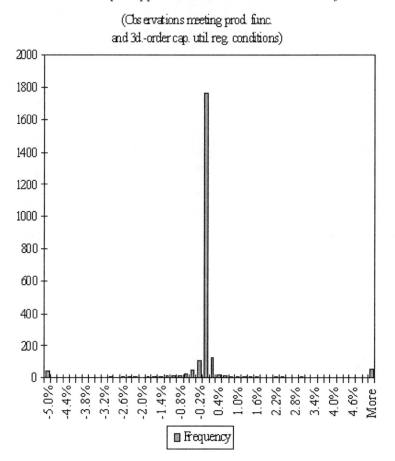

(Cbservations meeting prod. func.
and 3d.-order cap. util. reg. conditions)

TABLE 4.6. Mean output approximation error

(Observations meeting prod. func. and 3d.-order cap. util. reg. conditions)

Cou.	Num. Empl.	Year 1989	1990	1991	1992	1993	1994	1995	1996
Fr.	> 20,000	0.0%	0.0%	0.0%	0.0%	0.0%	0.0%	0.0%	0.0%
	4,000-20,000	-0.3%	-2.3%	-0.6%	-0.1%	-0.3%	0.0%	0.1%	0.7%
	< 4,000	-0.3%	-0.6%	-0.5%	-0.3%	0.4%	0.5%	44.2%	7.6%
Ger.	> 20,000	-0.8%	-0.3%	-0.5%	-0.2%	-0.2%	-0.1%	0.0%	0.1%
	4,000-20,000	-5.7%	-0.8%	-0.4%	-2.2%	-0.4%	-0.1%	0.2%	1.4%
	< 4,000	-1.2%	-2.7%	-2.5%	-2.9%	37.2%	5.3%	13.8%	9.2%
Jap.	> 20,000	0.0%	0.0%	0.0%	0.0%	0.0%	0.0%	0.0%	0.0%
	4,000-20,000	0.0%	0.0%	0.0%	0.0%	0.0%	0.0%	0.0%	0.0%
	< 4,000	-1.1%	-0.8%	-0.3%	-0.1%	0.6%	3.1%	4.6%	5.5%
UK	> 20,000	0.0%	0.0%	0.0%	0.0%	0.0%	0.0%	0.0%	0.0%
	4,000-20,000	0.0%	0.0%	0.0%	-0.7%	-0.1%	-0.6%	-0.3%	-1.1%
	< 4,000	-0.5%	0.0%	3.1%	-0.1%	-1.6%	-1.7%	6.9%	0.2%
US	> 20,000	0.0%	0.0%	0.0%	0.0%	0.0%	0.0%	0.0%	0.0%
	4,000-20,000	0.0%	-0.1%	0.0%	0.0%	0.0%	-0.1%	-0.1%	0.0%
	< 4,000	-0.6%	-0.8%	-0.6%	-0.4%	-0.5%	0.0%	1.2%	13.4%

Notice that small banks in latter years, which tend to have highly negative values of λ_{it}, usually have high output approximation errors.

Now, large absolute values of λ_{it} imply a need for approximation far away from the initial conditions and therefore should necessitate relatively high-order Taylor expansions, so that the issue could be hoped to be settled simply by adding a fourth-order term to the Taylor expansions for bothersome observations.

As it turns out, however, the pattern in Table 4.6 does not improve significantly when fourth-, and even fifth-order terms are added to the Taylor series. Is this situation due to the need to add even higher-order terms or is it due to the fact that the estimated production function does not provide an adequate approximation to the true production function in the relevant neighbourhood?

An examination of the regularity conditions suggests that the solution to this problem involves adding, where necessary, even higher-order terms to the Taylor expansions. Indeed, the third table in the Appendix, which presents for each sub-sample the percentage of data points meeting the regularity conditions for third-order Taylor approximations, indicates that most of the sub-samples which are problematic in an output approximation sense also have relatively low proportions of regular observations — clearly, the input levels estimated in these sub-samples are unreliable.

Focusing on third-order results for medium-sized and large banks, Table 4.7 provides the estimated labour capacity utilisation rates.[25]

TABLE 4.7. Mean value of φ^l

(Observations meeting prod. func. and 3d.-order cap. util. reg. conditions)

Country	Num. Empl.	1989	1990	1991	1992	1993	1994	1995	1996
France	> 20,000	0.99	0.98	0.95	0.90	0.83	0.78	0.69	0.62
	4,000-20,000	0.98	0.92	0.91	0.85	0.74	0.67	0.54	0.46
Germany	> 20,000	0.81	0.81	0.77	0.75	0.69	0.64	0.57	0.53
	4,000-20,000	0.78	0.82	0.82	0.68	0.72	0.68	0.54	0.51
Japan	> 20,000	1.12	1.07	1.04	0.99	0.95	0.92	0.84	0.86
	4,000-20,000	0.98	0.96	0.93	0.87	0.74	0.62	0.49	0.40
UK	> 20,000	1.00	1.00	1.02	0.98	0.93	0.87	0.81	0.76
	4,000-20,000	1.00	1.02	0.96	1.04	0.78	0.68	0.59	0.75
US	> 20,000	1.16	1.13	1.16	1.12	1.08	1.01	0.93	0.87
	4,000-20,000	1.10	1.16	1.16	1.13	1.05	0.95	0.84	0.72

The 1996 values of these labour capacity utilisation rates are generally quite low; consider for instance that a rate of 62% for large French banks suggests 38% excess employment, while a rate of 40% for medium-sized Japanese banks indicates a whopping 60% excess employment.

Table 4.8 reports the corresponding results for technology capacity utilisation rates. Notice that the 1996 values of the technology utilisation rates are larger than one, indicating insufficient technology spending, and are consistent with the corresponding labour capacity utilisation rates.

---

[25] Very similar capacity utilisation rates were obtained through the two-step econometric method proposed in Section 2.3.3. (with a translog specification of the shadow cost function). Results for the subset of small banks meeting the required regularity conditions are not reported since this subset is obviously biased in favour of observations with relatively small absolute values of the allocative efficiency index.

TABLE 4.8. Mean value of φ^t

(Observations meeting prod. func. and 3d.-order cap. util. reg. conditions)

Country	Num.Empl.	1989	1990	1991	1992	1993	1994	1995	1996
France	> 20,000	1.06	1.07	1.16	1.32	1.50	1.59	1.80	1.97
	4,000-20,000	1.27	1.56	1.55	1.54	1.86	1.90	2.23	2.62
Germany	> 20,000	2.38	2.21	2.40	2.26	2.46	2.40	2.50	2.52
	4,000-20,000	2.37	2.03	1.86	2.46	2.13	1.99	2.29	2.23
Japan	> 20,000	0.72	0.82	0.91	1.04	1.10	1.14	1.32	1.21
	4,000-20,000	1.07	1.10	1.17	1.31	1.58	1.78	1.98	1.91
UK	> 20,000	1.02	1.01	0.96	1.06	1.20	1.36	1.52	1.59
	4,000-20,000	1.01	0.99	1.15	1.34	1.73	2.24	2.41	1.93
US	> 20,000	0.65	0.78	0.71	0.79	0.88	1.01	1.14	1.33
	4,000-20,000	0.80	0.76	0.78	0.85	1.03	1.18	1.34	1.53

Considering carefully Tables 4.7 and 4.8, and comparing them with Table 4.5, a reasonably linear relation seems to exist between the input utilisation rates and the allocative efficiency indices as long as the absolute value of λ_{it} is close to zero. This is easily confirmed by plotting, as in Figure 4.14, labour utilisation rates as a function of λ_{it}.

In the neighbourhood of zero, the basic relation seems to be that a 0.5 decrease in λ_{it} yields a corresponding decrease in the labour capacity utilisation rate of approximately 0.35.

4.3.3   Economic Consequences

What are the cost consequences of sub-optimal capacity utilisation?

Naturally, the higher the absolute value of λ_{it}, the higher the induced cost surcharge. This is illustrated in Figure 4.15 which examines the first-order derivative of the cost/income ratio with respect to λ_{it}.

As expected, this Figure suggests that the original relation in levels is U-shaped, with a minimum at zero: cost is minimum when the factor mix is chosen optimally. This U-shaped pattern can be easily exhibited by examining the estimated individual cost surcharges as a function of λ_{it}, as in Figure 4.16.

FIGURE 4.14. φ^l vs. λ

(Observations meeting prod. func.
and 3d.-order cap. util. reg. conditions)

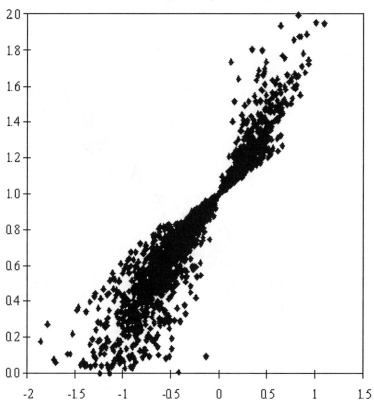

FIGURE 4.15. $\frac{\partial \xi}{\partial \lambda}$ vs. λ

(Observations meeting prod. func.
and 3d.-order cap. util. reg. conditions)

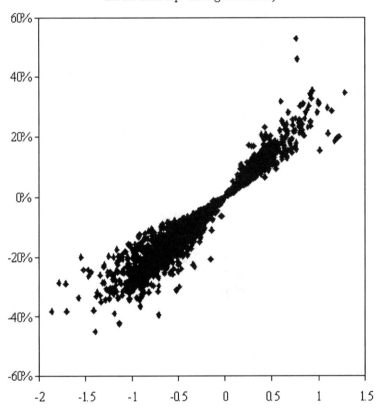

FIGURE 4.16. τ vs. λ

(Observations meeting prod. func.
and 3d.-order cap. utl. reg. conditions)

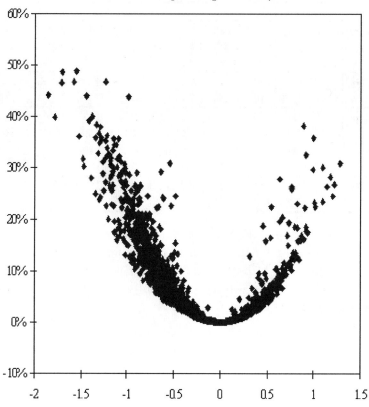

This pattern implies that the cost surcharge induced by disequilibrium accelerates when λ_{it} diverges from zero:[26] moving, for instance, from 0 to -0.5 should produce a much less dramatic cost increase than moving from -0.5 to -1.

A more precise and segmented insight into the economic consequences of disequilibrium is provided in Table 4.9, which reports the estimated cost surcharges by sub-sample.

TABLE 4.9. Mean value of τ

(Observations meeting prod. func. and 3d.-order cap. util. reg. conditions)

% of current cost	Year							
Cou.	Num. Empl.	1989	1990	1991	1992	1993	1994	1995	1996
Fr.	> 20,000	0.3%	0.3%	0.4%	1.1%	2.6%	3.9%	7.0%	10.0%
	4,000-20,000	2.1%	4.3%	3.7%	3.1%	6.1%	7.8%	13.6%	18.8%
Ger.	> 20,000	4.6%	4.4%	6.0%	6.3%	9.3%	11.1%	14.2%	16.6%
	4,000-20,000	6.9%	4.4%	4.1%	9.8%	9.7%	10.0%	15.0%	15.7%
Jap.	> 20,000	1.2%	0.5%	0.1%	0.0%	0.1%	0.4%	1.9%	1.1%
	4,000-20,000	0.1%	0.2%	0.5%	1.4%	4.1%	7.5%	12.0%	13.4%
UK	> 20,000	0.1%	0.1%	0.1%	0.2%	0.5%	2.1%	3.9%	5.1%
	4,000-20,000	0.2%	0.6%	0.6%	6.0%	5.1%	9.9%	12.6%	14.9%
US	> 20,000	3.0%	2.6%	3.1%	1.9%	1.2%	0.5%	0.8%	3.2%
	4,000-20,000	1.2%	2.7%	2.3%	2.2%	2.0%	2.2%	3.8%	6.7%

As expected, the 1996 cost surcharges are higher for French and German banks than for British and American banks, since the former have worse capacity utilisation rates — but it is important to realise that these cost surcharges are in virtually all cases quite material since they apply to the entire cost base.

---

[26] This fundamental non-linearity will appear again in the comparative statitics results presented later.

4.4   Impact of Labour Market Rigidities

Assume that the impact of European labour market rigidities is reflected in 1996 in the differences between the allocative efficiency indices in the United States and in Europe.[27]

It is then possible to estimate the stand-alone impact of these rigidities by forcing the 1996 values of the allocative efficiency indices of European banks to those for similar-sized US banks.

The results of this exercise, using third-order Taylor expansions, are summarised in Table 4.10.[28]

TABLE 4.10. Impact of labour market rigidities

Cou.	Num. Empl.	Excess Jobs (% of current jobs)	Excess Cost (% of current cost)	"Rigidity Tax" (% of notional pre-tax profit)*	Cost per "Saved" Job (1996 US doll.)
Fr.	> 20,000	26%	8.8%	31.9%	32,068
	4,000-20,000	33%	15.3%	41.6%	38,089
Ger.	> 20,000	37%	15.5%	33.9%	37,319
	4,000-20,000	26%	11.2%	27.8%	33,304
UK	> 20,000	12%	3.7%	6.6%	20,357
	4,000-20,000	11%	7.4%	16.0%	20,809

*Excluding one observation for Germany with negative n. p.-t. p.

The first two columns in Table 4.10 indicate that, keeping output levels constant,[29] labour market rigidities currently "protect" ~26-37% of the banking jobs in France and Germany, with a corresponding cost surcharge of ~9-16%.

In the third column of Table 4.10, this cost surcharge is considered an implicit "rigidity tax" and compared with notional pre-tax profit, i.e. the pre-tax profit that would prevail in the absence of rigidity.

---

[27] This is actually a conservative definition of the impact of labour market rigidities, which could also be defined to include the difference between the competitive wage level in the US and the artificially high wage levels in Europe.

[28] The production function and the capacity utilisation regularity conditions are used to screen for observations in Table 4.10. Notice however that, from a formal point of view, the capacity utilisation regularity conditions are not necessary here: weaker regularity conditions would suffice since the approximations are conducted closer to the initial values of the allocative efficiency indices.

[29] If labour market rigidities are removed, output may indeed increase as a consequence of the shifting of the supply curve (and thereby induce a corresponding increase in the demand for labour).

Interestingly, for French and German banks, this implicit "rigidity tax" turns out to be comparable to explicit corporate tax rates, in the 28-42% range.[30]

Finally, considering the situation from a public policy perspective, is the money efficiently spent? If banks are basically forced to run a private employment subsidy program, at their own expense, what is the cost per "protected" job? Quite high according to the estimates presented in the last column of Table 4.10 which indicate an average annual cost per "protected" job, imposed on the private sector, in the $32,000-$38,000 range for French and German banks.[31]

4.5   Sources of International Cost Position Differences

As discussed in Section 3.2, the presence of output price noise makes it impossible to identify the sources of cost differences through equation (2.24) unless the two observations to be compared can be assumed to involve identical output prices.

In the current context, this assumption is clearly unlikely to hold for comparisons:

- of observations at two different points in time, since the evidence in Section 4.1.4 confirms that latent output prices were generally dropping in the 1989-1996 period;

- involving banks of significantly different sizes, which in all likelihood have different output mixes, as discussed in Section 4.2.2;

- involving different small banks, since small banks tend to operate in focused geographic markets with a narrow product line, so that different small banks are unlikely to be operating under comparable market conditions.

This list is of course not exhaustive and, in the current context, no possible comparison is in fact entirely immune to criticisms of the validity of the assumption of identical output prices.

---

[30] This implicit tax obviously represents a significantly higher percentage of unadjusted pre-tax profit levels.

[31] These are 1996 US dollars at purchasing price parity.

These words of caution notwithstanding, Table 4.11 presents the results of a third-order accounting exercise on the 1996 differences in cost positions between large banks, using simple arithmetic means of the variables in (2.24).

TABLE 4.11. Sources of cost differences: first sub-sample

(Banks with > 20,000 employees;
1996 observations meeting prod. func. and 3d.-order cap. util. reg. cond.)

Cou.	Cost Diff. vs. US	Explained Effects	Prices	Scale	Efficiency	Cap. Util.	Cross- Terms	Resid. Effects
Fr.	11.5%		10.0%	0.0%	-4.3%	6.1%	-0.5%	0.3%
		1st.-order.	10.0%	0.0%	-4.3%	6.2%	na	
		2nd.-order.	0.0%	0.0%	0.0%	0.1%	-0.4%	
		3d.-order.	0.0%	0.0%	0.0%	-0.2%	-0.1%	
Ger.	5.0%		8.7%	-0.5%	-13.2%	10.8%	-0.9%	0.1%
		1st.-order.	8.7%	-0.5%	-13.1%	10.4%	na	
		2nd.-order.	0.0%	0.0%	0.0%	1.0%	0.1%	
		3d.-order.	0.0%	0.0%	-0.1%	-0.7%	-1.0%	
Jap.	-0.7%		4.9%	1.2%	-6.3%	-0.2%	0.0%	-0.2%
		1st.-order.	4.9%	1.2%	-6.3%	-0.2%	na	
		2nd.-order.	0.0%	0.0%	0.0%	0.0%	0.0%	
		3d.-order.	0.0%	0.0%	0.0%	0.0%	0.0%	
UK	-3.3%		2.3%	-5.3%	-1.4%	1.8%	0.0%	-0.8%
		1st.-order.	2.3%	-5.3%	-1.4%	1.8%	na	
		2nd.-order.	0.0%	-0.1%	0.0%	0.1%	0.1%	
		3d.-order.	0.0%	0.1%	0.0%	0.0%	-0.1%	

Notice first that the price effects referred to in Table 4.11 are of course due to differences in labour prices, since output and technology prices are identical by construction.

The small values of the unexplained residuals provide some evidence that output prices for large G-5 banks may have been relatively homogeneous in 1996 — but the results for Japan must be handled with care for the reasons discussed in Section 3.3.

The difference between large UK and US banks seems to be mostly due to sample composition effects as can be induced from the importance of the estimated scale effects. This is confirmed on closer examination: the average number of employees for the British sub-sample was ~69,000 versus ~44,000 for the American one.

More importantly, notice that the combination of price and capacity utilisation effects actually seems to more than explain the relatively unfavourable cost positions of large French and German banks: their relative cost/income ratios would in fact be significantly worse were it not for compensating technical efficiency effects.

Table 4.12 presents the results of a similar exercise for medium-sized banks.

TABLE 4.12. Sources of cost differences: second sub-sample

(Banks with 4,000-20,000 employees;
1996 observations meeting prod. func. and 3d.-order cap. util. reg. cond.)

Cou.	Cost Diff. vs. US	Explained Effects						Resid. Effects
			Prices	Scale	Efficiency	Cap. Util.	Cross-Terms	
Fr.	13.1%		7.9%	0.6%	-6.0%	9.9%	-0.7%	1.3%
		1st.-order.	7.9%	0.6%	-6.0%	10.0%	na	
		2nd.-order.	0.0%	0.0%	0.0%	0.2%	-0.3%	
		3d.-order.	0.0%	0.0%	0.0%	-0.2%	-0.3%	
Ger.	5.8%		6.7%	0.9%	-7.8%	5.8%	-0.3%	0.5%
		1st.-order.	6.7%	0.9%	-7.8%	5.8%	na	
		2nd.-order.	0.0%	0.0%	0.0%	0.1%	0.0%	
		3d.-order.	0.0%	0.0%	0.0%	-0.1%	-0.2%	
Jap.	2.3%		3.6%	-4.4%	-1.4%	5.0%	0.2%	-0.6%
		1st.-order.	3.5%	-4.6%	-1.4%	5.0%	na	
		2nd.-order.	0.0%	0.5%	0.0%	0.0%	0.1%	
		3d.-order.	0.0%	-0.3%	0.0%	0.0%	0.1%	
UK	3.8%		1.9%	0.6%	-3.5%	2.6%	-0.1%	2.2%
		1st.-order.	1.9%	0.6%	-3.5%	2.6%	na	
		2nd.-order.	0.0%	0.0%	0.0%	0.0%	0.0%	
		3d.-order.	0.0%	0.0%	0.0%	0.0%	-0.1%	

The unexplained residual effects are here somewhat larger than those in Table 4.11, possibly because of more significant output price differences.

The results for medium-sized Japanese banks seem dominated by sample composition effects: the average number of employees in the Japanese sub-sample does indeed turn out to be about half that in the American sub-sample.

Medium-sized UK banks seem to be in a situation comparable to that of medium-sized US banks, with modestly unfavourable price and capacity utilisation effects on the downside and a fairly favourable technical efficiency effect on the upside.

Finally, for French and German banks, the general effects in Table 4.12 seem consistent with those identified in Table 4.11, with the considerable cost handicap induced by price and capacity utilisation effects only partially compensated by technical efficiency effects.

5
Conclusion

From a conceptual perspective, this study shows that, if the primal characterisation of the firm's program is leveraged to the fullest extent, it is in fact possible to study not only production but also cost with a minimal baggage of untested assumptions on the technology and behaviour of firms.

The resulting Flexible Cost Model (FCM) is indeed conducive to modern econometric techniques and allows for a flexible specification not only of a common underlying production technology but also of firm-level heterogeneity in technical and allocative efficiency levels. FCM, which is in fact a generalised shadow cost model, nests both the traditional neo-classical cost model and a wide range of other models explicitly or implicitly imposing rigid assumptions on allocative inefficiency. FCM is also in some sense more flexible than parametric frontier models which require more a priori structure on firm-level technical efficiency.

When applied to situations in which firms may be unable or unwilling to optimise their factor mix, the proposed model allows the assessment of the impact on factor demand and on cost of all relevant underlying effects: price and scale effects, of course, but also technical efficiency and capacity utilisation effects.

From an empirical perspective, the current study focused on the G-5 banking industries in the 1989-1996 period. FCM was found to be essentially robust to the type of output measurement issues which complicate banking research, and four basic issues were examined:

- Does FCM account better than more restrictive models for the behaviour of G-5 banks in the 1989-1996 period?

- Does FCM provide any new evidence as to the existence of scale economies for large banks?

- What is the nature and extent of disequilibrium in general, and of disequilibrium induced by labour market rigidities in particular?

- What are the sources of the current performance gap between, on the one hand, American and British banks and, on the other hand, French and German banks?

With respect to the first question, the answer is unambiguously positive: statistical tests decisively reject both the neo-classical hypothesis and the assumptions maintained in previous, more restrictive shadow cost models. At least in the current context, FCM can be considered a meaningful generalisation of previously proposed approaches, and more restrictive models may lead to inaccurate inferences with respect to firm technology and firm behaviour.

With respect to scale effects, the conclusions of this study are different from those of most (but not all) previous cost function based studies, which may have suffered from modelling and econometric biases. More specifically, this study indicates that banks with more than ~10,000 employees enjoy significant and increasing scale economies, while smaller banks suffer from scale diseconomies. Ceteris paribus, as a bank evolves in size from ~2,500 to ~10,000 employees, its cost/income ratio seems to increase by about 19%, and a multiplication of size by ten, from ~10,000 to ~100,000 employees, is necessary for the cost/income ratio to drop back to its initial level. This inverted U-shaped pattern, which provides some microeconomic foundation to the current wave of merger activity in banking, may reflect the need for banks, as they get larger, to evolve from low to high fixed-cost technological infrastructures that must be leveraged on large customer bases.

Concerning disequilibrium, this study concludes that G-5 banks, especially Continental European and smaller banks, suffer increasingly from excess labour. Focusing for instance on banks with more than ~20,000 employees, the 1996 estimated labour capacity utilisation rates point to ~14-24% excess labour in the United States, in the United Kingdom and in Japan, versus ~38-47% in France and Germany; the corresponding cost surcharges are ~1-5% and ~10-17%.

The impact of labour market rigidities in Continental Europe is estimated to be considerable. For French and German banks with more than 20,000 employees, these rigidities are estimated to "protect" in 1996 ~26-37% of banking jobs, and to induce excess costs that represent an annual ~$32,000-37,000 per "protected" job and amount to an implicit "rigidity tax" in the ~32-34% range — a range comparable to that of explicit corporate tax rates.

Finally, despite data limitations, the relative uncompetitiveness of the cost position of French and German banks appears to be entirely due to higher labour prices and worse capacity utilisation rates, presumably as a consequence of labour market rigidities.

****

The empirical conclusions of this study need to be placed in a broader context.

As argued in Section 3.1, banking can be considered a prototypical service activity and much of the patterns here discussed are also likely to apply to the many other service activities that are being transformed by the information technology revolution.

Given the relatively low estimated labour capacity utilisation rates in banking and the likely continued decline in the relative price of information technology, this study suggests that the process of technology-for-labour substitution is merely beginning in very substantial parts of the G-5 economies.

In countries with flexible labour markets, massive job losses should be expected in the coming years not only in banking but also in insurance, in government and in the ranks of the clerical staff that today account for a considerable portion of the employment in other service sectors and in manufacturing.

In the advanced economies of the 21st century, paper-based information processing will probably be no more common than plow-based agriculture; in a new episode of Schumpeterian creative destruction, entire industries will have been decimated and new ones will have emerged.

If history and economic theory are any guide, tomorrow's advanced economies will be those which today offer environments conducive to the emergence of these new industries — environments which include competitive product, labour and capital markets, non-punitive taxation rates, limited regulatory impediments and liberal trade policies.

Current labour market rigidities in Continental Europe, by protecting jobs and wage levels in dying industries, therefore do not only hurt the short-term competitiveness of national firms, as indicated in this study, but also prevent the migration of employment towards the wealth-creating industries of the future.

6
Bibliography

Arellano, M. "Some Testing for Autocorrelation in Dynamic Random Effects Models." *Review of Economics Studies*, 1990, *57*, pp. 127-134.

Arellano, M. "On the Testing of Correlated Effects with Panel Data." *Journal of Econometrics*, 1991, *59*, pp. 87-97.

Arellano, M. and Bond, S. "Some Tests of Specification for Panel Data: Monte Carlo Evidence and an Application to Employment Equations." *Review of Economics Studies*, 1991, *58*, pp. 29-51.

Arellano, M. and Bover, O. "Another Look at the Instrumental Variables Estimation of Error Components Models." *Journal of Econometrics*, 1995, *68*, pp. 29-51.

Arrow, K.J. and Chenerey, H.B. and Minhas, B.S. and Solow, R.W. "Capital-Labor Substitution and Economic Efficiency." *The Review of Economics and Statistics*, 1961, *3*, pp. 225-250.

Arrow, Kenneth J. and Enthoven, Alain. "Quasiconcave Programming." *Econometrica*, 1961, *4*, pp. 779-800.

Arrow, Kenneth J. and Hurwicz, Leonid and Uzawa, Hirofumi. "Constraint Qualification in Maximization Problems." *Naval Research Logistics Quarterly*, 1961, *2*, pp. 175-191.

Baltagi, Badi H. *Econometric Analysis of Panel Data.* New York: John Wiley and Sons, 1995.

Barnett, William A. and Lee, Yul W. "The Global Properties of the Minflex Laurent, Generalized Leontief, and Translog Flexible Functional Forms." *Econometrica*, 1985, *53*, pp. 1421-1437.

Bauer, Paul W. and Berger, Allen N. and Humphrey, David B. "Inefficiency and Productivity Growth in Banking: A Comparison of Stochastic Econometric and Thick Frontier Methods." *Working Paper Series.* Federal Reserve Bank of Cleveland, 1991, *no. 9117.*

Bell, Frederick W. and Murphy, Neil B. *Costs in Commercial Banking.* Boston: Federal Reserve Bank of Boston, 1968.

Benston, George J. "Economies of Scale and Marginal Costs in Banking Operations." *The National Banking Review*, 1965, *2*, pp. 507-549.

Benston, George J. and Hanweck, Gerald A. and Humphrey, David B. "Scale Economics in Banking: A Restructuring and Reassessment." *Journal of Money, Credit and Banking*, 1982, *14*, pp. 435-456.

Berger, Allen N. and Hanweck, Gerald A. and Humphrey, David B. "Competitive Viability in Banking: Scale, Scope, and Product Mix Economies." *Journal of Monetary Economics*, 1987, *20*, pp. 501-520.

Berger, Allen N. and Humphrey, David B. "Efficiency of Financial Institutions: International Survey and Directions for Future Research." *Working Paper Series.* The Wharton School, University of Pennsylvania, 1997, *no. 97-05.*

Berndt, Ernst R. and Hesse, Dieter M. "Measuring and Assessing Capacity Utilization in the Manufacturing

Sectors of Nine OECD Countries." *European Economic Review*, 1986, *30*, pp. 961-989.

Berndt, Ernst R. and Morrison, Catherine J. "Capacity Utilization Measures: Underlying Economic Theory and an Alternative Approach" in *Papers and Proceedings of the Ninety-Third Annual Meeting of the American Economic Association,* Nashville: American Economic Review, 1980, pp. 48-52.

Blundell, Richard and Bond, Stephen. "Initial Conditions and Moment Restrictions in Dynamic Panel Data Models." *Discussion Paper No. 104.* Oxford: Nuffield College, 1995.

Bregman, Arie and Fuss, Melvyn and Regev, Haim. "The Production and Cost Structure of Israeli Industry: Evidence from Individual Firm Data." *Journal of Econometrics*, 1995, *65*, pp. 45-81.

Carrington, Mark, Langguth, Philip and Steiner, Thomas. *The Banking Revolution.* London: Business FT Pitman Publishing, 1997.

Christensen, L.R. and Caves, D. W. "Global Properties of Flexible Functional Forms." *American Economic Review*, 1980, *70*, pp. 322-332.

Christensen, L.R and Jorgensen, D.W.and Lau, L.J. "Transcendental Logarithmic Production Frontiers." *Econometrica*, 1973, *55*, pp. 28-45.

Diewert, W.E. and Wales, T.J. "Flexible Functional Forms and Global Curvature Conditions." *Econometrica*, 1987, *1*, pp. 43-68.

Diewert, W.E. "Applications of Duality Theory" in *Frontiers of Quantitative Economics*, ed. by M.D. Intrilligator and D.A. Kendrick. Amsterdam: North Holland, 1974, pp. 106-171.

Diewert, W.E. "An Application of the Shephard Duality Theorem: A Generalized Leontief Production Function." *Journal of Political Economy*, 1971, *79*, pp. 481-507.

Evanoff, Douglas D. and Israilevich, Philip R. and Merris, Randall. C. "Relative Price Efficiency, Technical Change and Scale Economies for Large Commercial Banks." *Journal of Regulatory Economics*, 1990, *2*, pp. 281-298.

Färe, Rolf and Primont, Daniel. *Multi-Output Production and Duality: Theory and Applications.* Boston: Kluwer Academic Publishers, 1995.

Forsund, Finn R. and Lovell, C.A. Knox and Schmidt, Peter. "A Survey of Frontier Production Functions and of their Relationship to Efficiency Measurement." *Journal of Econometrics*, 1980, *13*, pp. 5-25.

Gallant, Ronald A. and Golub, Gene H. "Imposing Curvature Restrictions on Flexible Forms." *Journal of Econometrics*, 1984, *13*, pp. 295-321.

Gilbert, Alton R. "Bank Market Structure and Competition: A Survey." *Journal of Money, Credit and Banking*, 1984, *16*, pp. 617-645.

Gilligan, Thomas and Smirlock Michael. "An Empirical Study of Joint Production and Scale Economies in Commercial Banking." *Journal of Banking and Finance*, 1984, *8*, pp. 67-76.

Gilligan, Thomas and Smirlock, Michael and Marshall, William. "Scale and Scope Economies in the Multiproduct Banking Firm." *Journal of Monetary Economics*, 1984, *13*, pp. 393-405.

Green, William H. *Econometric Analysis.* New Jersey: Prentice Hall, 1997.

Griliches, Zvi and Mairesse, Jacques. "Comparing Productivity Growth: An Exploration of French and U.S. Industrial Firm Data." *European Economic Review*, 1983, *21*, pp. 89-119.

Griliches, Zvi and Mairesse, Jacques. "Heterogeneity in Panel Data: Are there Stable Production Functions?" in *Essays in Honor of Edmond Malinvaud, vol. 3*, ed. by Paul Champsaur et. al. Cambridge: MIT Press, 1990, pp. 193-231.

Griliches, Zvi and Mairesse, Jacques. "R&D and Productivity Growth: Comparing Japanese and U.S. Manufacturing Firms" in *Productivity Growth in Japan and the United States*, ed. by Charles R. Hulten. Chicago: University of Chicago Press, 1990, pp. 317-340.

Hall, Bronwyn H. and Mairesse, Jacques. "Exploring the Relationship between R&D and Productivity in French Manufacturing Firms." *Journal of Econometrics*, 1995, *65*, pp. 263-293.

Hardy, G.H. and Littlewood, J.E. and Polya, G. *Inequalities.* Cambridge: Cambridge University Press, 1934.

Henderson, James M. and Quandt, Richard E. *Microeconomic Theory: A Mathematical Approach.* New York: McGraw Hill, 1980.

Hsiao, Cheng. *Analysis of Panel Data.* Cambridge: Cambridge University Press, 1986.

Hunter, William C. and Timme, Stephen G. "Technical Change, Organizational Form and the Structure of Bank Production." *Journal of Money, Credit and Banking*, 1986, *18*, pp. 152-166.

Hunter, William and Timme, Stephen. "Technical Change in Large U.S. Commercial Banks." *Working Paper Series.* Federal Reserve Bank of Atlanta, 1988, *no. 88-6.*

Hunter, William and Timme, Stephen. "International Comparisons of Bank Production Characteristics and Technological Change." *Applied Economics*, 1992, *24*, pp. 45-57.

Kaparakis, Emmanuel I. and Miller, Stephen M. and Noulas, Athanasios G. "Short-Run Cost Inefficiency in Commercial Banks: A Flexible Stochastic Frontier Approach." *Journal of Money, Credit and Banking*, 1994, *26*, pp. 875-893.

Kolari, James and Zardkoohi, Ashgar. *Bank Costs, Structure, and Performance.* Lexington, D.C.: Heath and Company, 1987.

McFadden, Daniel. "Cost, Revenue and Profit Functions" in *Production Economics: A Dual Approach to Theory and Applications*, ed. by M. Fuss and D. McFadden. Amsterdam: North Holland, 1978, pp. 3-109.

Lau, L.J. and Yotopoulos, P.A. "A Test for Relative Efficiency and Application to Indian Agriculture." *American Economic Review*, 1971, *61*, pp. 94-109.

Lau, L.J. "Testing and Imposing Monotonicity, Convexity and Quasiconvexity Constraints" in *Production Economics: A Dual Approach to Theory and Applications*, ed. by M. Fuss and D. McFadden. Amsterdam: North Holland, 1978, pp. 409-453.

Luenberger, David G. *Microeconomic Theory.* New York: McGraw Hill, 1995.

Mairesse, Jacques and Kremp, Elizabeth. "A Look at Productivity at the Firm Level in Eight French Service Industries." *The Journal of Productivity Analysis*, 1993, *4*, pp. 211-234.

Morrison, C.J. and Berndt, E.R. "Short-Run Labor Productivity in a Dynamic Model." *Journal of Econometrics*, 1981, *16*, pp. 339-365.

Morrison, Catherine J. "Primal and Dual Capacity Utilization: An Application to Productivity Measurement in the U.S. Automobile Industry." *Journal of Business & Economic Statistics*, 1985, *4*, pp. 312-324.

Olley, G. Steven and Pakes, Ariel. "The Dynamics of Productivity in the Telecommunications Industry." *Econometrica*, 1996, *6*, pp. 1263-1297.

Reiman, Mark A. "Shortage Intensity, Priority Penetration, and Resource Allocation in Socialist Industry: A Translog Cost Model." *Journal of Comparative Economics*, 1994, *19*, pp. 237-259.

Shaffer, Sherrill. "Scale Economies in Multiproduct Firms." *Bulletin of Economic Research*, 1984, *36*, pp. 51-58.

Steiner, Thomas D. and Teixeira, Diego. *Technology in Banking.* Homewood, Illinois: Business One Irwin, 1990.

Toda, Yasushi. "Estimation of a Cost Function when the Cost is Not Minimum: the Case of Soviet Manufacturing Industries, 1958-1971." *Review of Economics and Statistics*, 1976, *3*, pp. 259-268.

Varian, Hal R. *Microeconomic Analysis.* New York: W.W. Norton & Company, 1992.

Wiley, D. and Schmidt, W.H. and Bramble W.J. "Studies of a Class of Covariance Structure Models." *Journal of the American Statistical Society*, 1973, *68*, pp. 317-323.

William A. and Lee, Yul W. "The Global Properties of the Minflex Laurent, Generalized Leontief, and Translog Flexible Functional Forms." *Econometrica*, 1985, *53*, pp. 1421-1437.

7
Appendix: Dataset Statistics

TABLE 7.1. Number of observations by sub-sample

Cou.	Num. Empl.	Year 1989	1990	1991	1992	1993	1994	1995	1996	Total
Fr.	> 20,000	7	8	9	8	8	8	8	4	60
	4,000-20,000	9	8	7	10	9	9	7	5	64
	< 4,000	12	15	16	21	28	24	20	15	151
France Sample		28	31	32	39	45	41	35	24	275
Ger.	> 20,000	3	3	4	4	4	4	4	3	29
	4,000-20,000	6	6	5	6	8	8	8	7	54
	< 4,000	14	14	18	19	20	22	17	11	135
Germany Sample		23	23	27	29	32	34	29	21	218
Jap.	> 20,000	1	2	2	2	2	2	2	2	15
	4,000-20,000	6	6	6	6	8	8	8	7	55
	< 4,000	65	72	74	76	77	77	76	78	595
Japan Sample		72	80	82	84	87	87	86	87	665
UK	> 20,000	5	5	6	7	8	9	9	8	57
	4,000-20,000	3	3	4	8	11	11	8	8	56
	< 4,000	2	3	4	7	11	12	15	7	61
UK Sample		10	11	14	22	30	32	32	23	174
US	> 20,000	8	8	8	18	20	24	29	8	123
	4,000-20,000	33	36	36	101	110	106	95	33	550
	< 4,000	64	64	66	127	124	130	134	64	773
US Sample		105	108	110	246	254	260	258	105	1446
Total		238	253	265	420	448	454	440	260	2778

TABLE 7.2. Observations meeting prod. func. reg. cond.

Cou.	Num. Empl.	Year								Total
		1989	1990	1991	1992	1993	1994	1995	1996	
Fr.	> 20,000	100%	100%	100%	100%	100%	100%	100%	100%	100%
	4,000-20,000	100%	100%	100%	100%	100%	100%	100%	100%	100%
	< 4,000	83%	87%	88%	86%	82%	88%	85%	60%	83%
France Sample		93%	94%	94%	92%	89%	93%	91%	75%	91%
Ger.	> 20,000	100%	100%	100%	100%	100%	100%	100%	100%	100%
	4,000-20,000	83%	83%	100%	100%	100%	100%	100%	100%	96%
	< 4,000	93%	93%	83%	79%	85%	95%	82%	91%	87%
Germany Sample		91%	91%	89%	86%	91%	97%	90%	95%	91%
Jap.	> 20,000	100%	100%	100%	100%	100%	100%	100%	100%	100%
	4,000-20,000	100%	100%	100%	100%	100%	100%	100%	100%	100%
	< 4,000	94%	94%	99%	100%	100%	100%	100%	100%	98%
Japan Sample		94%	95%	99%	100%	100%	100%	100%	100%	99%
UK	> 20,000	100%	100%	100%	100%	100%	100%	100%	100%	100%
	4,000-20,000	100%	100%	100%	100%	100%	100%	100%	100%	100%
	< 4,000	100%	67%	75%	86%	82%	83%	80%	71%	80%
UK Sample		100%	91%	93%	95%	93%	94%	91%	91%	93%
US	> 20,000	100%	100%	100%	100%	100%	100%	100%	100%	100%
	4,000-20,000	100%	100%	100%	100%	100%	100%	100%	100%	100%
	< 4,000	98%	98%	97%	98%	98%	98%	88%	80%	95%
US Sample		99%	99%	98%	99%	99%	99%	94%	88%	97%
Total		96%	96%	97%	97%	97%	98%	94%	92%	96%

TABLE 7.3. Observations meeting all reg. cond.
(prod. func. and 3d.-order cap. util. reg. cond.)

Cou.	Num. Empl.	Year 1989	1990	1991	1992	1993	1994	1995	1996	Total
Fr.	> 20,000	100%	100%	100%	100%	100%	100%	100%	100%	100%
	4,000-20,000	100%	100%	100%	100%	100%	100%	100%	100%	100%
	< 4,000	75%	80%	75%	76%	71%	67%	45%	20%	64%
France Sample		89%	90%	88%	87%	82%	80%	69%	50%	80%
Ger.	> 20,000	100%	100%	100%	100%	100%	100%	100%	100%	100%
	4,000-20,000	83%	83%	80%	100%	100%	100%	100%	100%	94%
	< 4,000	50%	57%	67%	63%	55%	45%	18%	18%	48%
Germany Sample		65%	70%	74%	76%	72%	65%	52%	57%	67%
Jap.	> 20,000	100%	100%	100%	100%	100%	100%	100%	100%	100%
	4,000-20,000	100%	100%	100%	100%	100%	100%	100%	100%	100%
	< 4,000	91%	88%	91%	95%	92%	78%	39%	14%	73%
Japan Sample		92%	89%	91%	95%	93%	80%	47%	23%	76%
UK	> 20,000	100%	100%	100%	100%	100%	100%	100%	100%	100%
	4,000-20,000	100%	100%	100%	100%	91%	100%	100%	100%	98%
	< 4,000	100%	67%	75%	71%	73%	67%	60%	29%	64%
UK Sample		100%	91%	93%	91%	87%	88%	81%	78%	87%
US	> 20,000	100%	100%	100%	100%	100%	100%	100%	100%	100%
	4,000-20,000	100%	100%	100%	100%	100%	100%	100%	100%	100%
	< 4,000	89%	89%	89%	93%	91%	91%	75%	50%	85%
US Sample		93%	94%	94%	96%	96%	95%	87%	70%	92%
Total		90%	89%	90%	94%	92%	88%	75%	52%	84%

TABLE 7.4. Selected firm-level statistics: France

BANK	YEAR	EMPL.	κ	λ	φ^l	φ^t	τ
Banque Nationale de Paris	1989	54,867	1.20	-0.18	0.94	1.25	0.4%
Banque Nationale de Paris	1990	56,989	1.21	-0.23	0.92	1.31	0.7%
Banque Nationale de Paris	1991	55,591	1.21	-0.28	0.90	1.37	1.1%
Banque Nationale de Paris	1992	54,990	1.22	-0.45	0.83	1.62	2.8%
Banque Nationale de Paris	1993	52,641	1.22	-0.61	0.76	1.84	5.1%
Banque Nationale de Paris	1994	51,654	1.23	-0.75	0.69	2.02	7.7%
Banque Nationale de Paris	1995	48,618	1.23	-0.96	0.60	2.36	12.6%
Banque Nationale de Paris	1996	43,873	1.23	-1.10	0.52	2.51	16.6%
Cent. Nat. Caisses d'Epargne	1991	32,334	1.14	-0.04	0.98	1.05	0.0%
Cent. Nat. Caisses d'Epargne	1992	34,444	1.16	-0.23	0.90	1.27	0.8%
Cent. Nat. Caisses d'Epargne	1993	33,550	1.16	-0.40	0.82	1.49	2.5%
Cent. Nat. Caisses d'Epargne	1994	33,511	1.17	-0.49	0.77	1.58	3.7%
Comp. Financière de Paribas	1989	32,097	1.13	0.12	1.05	0.87	0.2%
Comp. Financière de Paribas	1990	32,688	1.14	0.07	1.03	0.92	0.1%
Comp. Financière de Paribas	1991	32,679	1.14	-0.18	0.93	1.23	0.5%
Comp. Financière de Paribas	1992	31,422	1.14	-0.24	0.90	1.28	0.8%
Comp. Financière de Paribas	1993	33,618	1.16	-0.49	0.79	1.62	3.5%
Comp. Financière de Paribas	1994	32,628	1.17	-0.50	0.77	1.59	3.8%
Comp. Financière de Paribas	1995	32,678	1.18	-0.57	0.72	1.64	5.2%
Comp. Financière de Paribas	1996	32,419	1.19	-0.78	0.61	1.88	9.4%
Compagnie Financière de CIC	1989	27,549	1.09	-0.25	0.91	1.39	0.9%
Compagnie Financière de CIC	1990	26,045	1.09	-0.29	0.89	1.43	1.2%
Compagnie Financière de CIC	1991	25,355	1.09	-0.30	0.88	1.42	1.3%
Compagnie Financière de CIC	1992	23,689	1.09	-0.41	0.83	1.55	2.5%
Compagnie Financière de CIC	1993	22,221	1.09	-0.52	0.76	1.68	4.2%
Compagnie Financière de CIC	1994	22,125	1.10	-0.69	0.68	1.90	7.2%
Compagnie Financière de CIC	1995	21,219	1.10	-0.93	0.56	2.28	13.0%
Crédit Agricole CA (AGGR)	1989	69,687	1.25	0.08	1.03	0.91	0.1%
Crédit Agricole CA (AGGR)	1990	69,950	1.25	0.04	1.02	0.95	0.0%
Crédit Agricole CA (AGGR)	1991	70,119	1.26	0.04	1.02	0.96	0.0%

TABLE 7.4. Selected firm-level statistics: France (cont'd)

BANK	YEAR	EMPL.	κ	λ	φ^l	φ^t	τ
Crédit Agricole CA (AGGR)	1992	69,132	1.27	-0.08	0.97	1.09	0.1%
Crédit Agricole CA (AGGR)	1993	65,440	1.27	-0.22	0.90	1.24	0.7%
Crédit Agricole CA (AGGR)	1994	65,258	1.28	-0.34	0.85	1.37	1.8%
Crédit Agricole CA (AGGR)	1995	63,780	1.29	-0.46	0.78	1.49	3.3%
Crédit Lyonnais	1989	58,399	1.21	-0.15	0.95	1.20	0.3%
Crédit Lyonnais	1990	61,794	1.23	-0.09	0.97	1.11	0.1%
Crédit Lyonnais	1991	64,842	1.24	-0.15	0.94	1.18	0.3%
Crédit Lyonnais	1992	61,906	1.25	-0.20	0.92	1.23	0.6%
Crédit Lyonnais	1993	68,224	1.28	-0.28	0.88	1.31	1.1%
Crédit Lyonnais	1994	64,081	1.28	-0.25	0.88	1.26	1.0%
Crédit Lyonnais	1995	56,745	1.27	-0.52	0.76	1.57	4.1%
Crédit Lyonnais	1996	50,863	1.27	-0.62	0.69	1.66	6.0%
Crédit Mutuel (AGGR)	1990	20,229	1.06	0.06	1.03	0.93	0.1%
Crédit Mutuel (AGGR)	1991	20,530	1.07	-0.07	0.97	1.08	0.1%
Crédit Mutuel (AGGR)	1995	20,513	1.11	-0.60	0.68	1.68	6.0%
Groupe des Banques Pop.	1989	24,080	1.09	0.15	1.06	0.83	0.3%
Groupe des Banques Pop.	1990	23,507	1.09	0.10	1.04	0.89	0.2%
Groupe des Banques Pop.	1991	22,788	1.09	0.03	1.01	0.97	0.0%
Groupe des Banques Pop.	1992	22,363	1.09	-0.21	0.91	1.24	0.7%
Groupe des Banques Pop.	1993	20,977	1.09	-0.35	0.83	1.41	2.0%
Groupe des Banques Pop.	1994	21,177	1.10	-0.50	0.75	1.58	4.0%
Groupe des Banques Pop.	1995	20,962	1.11	-0.65	0.66	1.76	7.0%
Société Générale	1989	47,304	1.19	0.00	1.00	1.00	0.0%
Société Générale	1990	46,783	1.19	-0.04	0.98	1.05	0.0%
Société Générale	1991	48,146	1.20	-0.14	0.95	1.16	0.3%
Société Générale	1992	46,122	1.20	-0.21	0.91	1.25	0.6%
Société Générale	1993	46,399	1.21	-0.34	0.85	1.40	1.7%
Société Générale	1994	44,945	1.22	-0.39	0.82	1.43	2.3%
Société Générale	1995	44,800	1.23	-0.54	0.74	1.59	4.4%
Société Générale	1996	47,198	1.25	-0.73	0.65	1.82	8.1%

TABLE 7.5. Selected firm-level statistics: Germany

BANK	YEAR	EMPL.	κ	λ	φ^l	φ^t	τ
Bayerische Vereinsbank AG	1991	20,065	1.03	-0.77	0.71	2.88	8.7%
Bayerische Vereinsbank AG	1992	22,131	1.06	-0.76	0.72	2.46	7.8%
Bayerische Vereinsbank AG	1993	21,807	1.07	-0.93	0.64	2.72	11.5%
Bayerische Vereinsbank AG	1994	21,734	1.09	-0.96	0.59	2.54	12.9%
Bayerische Vereinsbank AG	1995	21,290	1.10	-1.08	0.52	2.64	16.5%
Commerzbank AG	1989	27,817	1.07	-0.56	0.80	2.43	5.0%
Commerzbank AG	1990	28,433	1.08	-0.62	0.78	2.41	5.3%
Commerzbank AG	1991	29,485	1.09	-0.66	0.77	2.33	5.7%
Commerzbank AG	1992	30,567	1.11	-0.66	0.76	2.15	5.8%
Commerzbank AG	1993	31,703	1.13	-0.86	0.68	2.49	9.6%
Commerzbank AG	1994	29,158	1.13	-0.89	0.63	2.35	10.9%
Commerzbank AG	1995	29,939	1.15	-0.94	0.59	2.31	12.6%
Commerzbank AG	1996	28,074	1.15	-1.20	0.47	2.74	19.8%
Deutsche Bank AG	1989	59,217	1.19	-0.62	0.80	2.51	5.1%
Deutsche Bank AG	1990	68,112	1.22	-0.60	0.81	2.22	4.3%
Deutsche Bank AG	1991	74,824	1.24	-0.57	0.82	2.00	3.9%
Deutsche Bank AG	1992	78,358	1.26	-0.54	0.82	1.82	3.6%
Deutsche Bank AG	1993	81,161	1.28	-0.67	0.76	2.00	5.8%
Deutsche Bank AG	1994	77,422	1.29	-0.75	0.71	2.05	7.5%
Deutsche Bank AG	1995	78,106	1.30	-0.95	0.63	2.33	11.6%
Deutsche Bank AG	1996	78,599	1.32	-0.96	0.60	2.23	12.4%
Dresdner Bank AG	1989	37,579	1.12	-0.53	0.82	2.21	3.9%
Dresdner Bank AG	1990	38,600	1.13	-0.52	0.83	2.00	3.5%
Dresdner Bank AG	1991	40,998	1.14	-0.69	0.77	2.40	5.9%
Dresdner Bank AG	1992	44,752	1.17	-0.82	0.72	2.61	8.2%
Dresdner Bank AG	1993	44,558	1.18	-0.91	0.67	2.64	10.3%
Dresdner Bank AG	1994	42,134	1.19	-1.02	0.61	2.68	13.2%
Dresdner Bank AG	1995	42,598	1.20	-1.11	0.56	2.72	15.9%
Dresdner Bank AG	1996	42,975	1.22	-1.14	0.51	2.60	17.4%

TABLE 7.6. Selected firm-level statistics: Japan

BANK	YEAR	EMPL.	κ	λ	φ^l	φ^t	τ
Dai-Ichi Kangyo Bank	1989	23,487	1.09	0.28	1.12	0.72	1.2%
Dai-Ichi Kangyo Bank	1990	25,976	1.11	0.19	1.08	0.80	0.6%
Dai-Ichi Kangyo Bank	1991	25,969	1.11	0.13	1.06	0.87	0.3%
Dai-Ichi Kangyo Bank	1992	26,691	1.12	-0.01	1.00	1.01	0.0%
Dai-Ichi Kangyo Bank	1993	26,686	1.13	-0.11	0.95	1.11	0.2%
Dai-Ichi Kangyo Bank	1994	27,091	1.15	-0.14	0.92	1.14	0.3%
Dai-Ichi Kangyo Bank	1995	27,502	1.17	-0.18	0.90	1.17	0.6%
Dai-Ichi Kangyo Bank	1996	27,746	1.19	-0.13	0.92	1.11	0.3%
Sakura Bank Ltd	1990	31,265	1.13	0.16	1.07	0.83	0.4%
Sakura Bank Ltd	1991	31,249	1.14	0.05	1.02	0.95	0.0%
Sakura Bank Ltd	1992	31,048	1.14	-0.06	0.97	1.06	0.1%
Sakura Bank Ltd	1993	31,142	1.16	-0.08	0.96	1.08	0.1%
Sakura Bank Ltd	1994	30,834	1.17	-0.15	0.92	1.15	0.4%
Sakura Bank Ltd	1995	30,993	1.18	-0.45	0.77	1.48	3.3%
Sakura Bank Ltd	1996	30,207	1.19	-0.34	0.81	1.32	2.0%

TABLE 7.7. Selected firm-level statistics: UK

BANK	YEAR	EMPL.	κ	λ	φ^l	φ^t	τ
Barclays Bank Plc	1992	102,036	1.32	-0.13	0.95	1.15	0.2%
Barclays Bank Plc	1993	102,632	1.33	-0.21	0.92	1.23	0.6%
Barclays Bank Plc	1994	93,892	1.33	-0.48	0.81	1.58	3.2%
Barclays Bank Plc	1995	94,141	1.34	-0.59	0.75	1.70	4.9%
Barclays Bank Plc	1996	101,226	1.36	-0.70	0.70	1.80	6.9%
Barclays plc	1989	97,359	1.29	0.00	1.00	1.00	0.0%
Barclays plc	1990	96,576	1.30	0.04	1.01	0.96	0.0%
Barclays plc	1991	101,393	1.31	0.05	1.02	0.95	0.0%
Barclays plc	1992	102,036	1.32	-0.12	0.95	1.14	0.2%
Barclays plc	1993	102,632	1.33	-0.25	0.90	1.29	0.9%
Barclays plc	1994	93,892	1.33	-0.48	0.81	1.58	3.2%
Barclays plc	1995	94,141	1.34	-0.56	0.77	1.65	4.4%
Barclays plc	1996	99,304	1.36	-0.70	0.70	1.81	6.9%
HSBC Holdings Plc	1991	40,660	1.17	0.08	1.03	0.91	0.1%
HSBC Holdings Plc	1992	74,381	1.28	0.11	1.04	0.89	0.2%
HSBC Holdings Plc	1993	94,129	1.32	-0.09	0.96	1.10	0.1%
HSBC Holdings Plc	1994	92,701	1.33	-0.39	0.84	1.45	2.2%
HSBC Holdings Plc	1995	91,768	1.33	-0.69	0.72	1.86	6.5%
HSBC Holdings Plc	1996	102,281	1.36	-0.79	0.67	1.95	8.5%
Lloyds Bank plc	1989	63,727	1.23	-0.04	0.99	1.05	0.0%
Lloyds Bank plc	1990	65,728	1.23	-0.10	0.97	1.13	0.1%
Lloyds Bank plc	1991	59,455	1.23	-0.02	0.99	1.02	0.0%
Lloyds Bank plc	1992	57,168	1.23	-0.17	0.94	1.20	0.4%
Lloyds Bank plc	1993	50,526	1.22	-0.18	0.92	1.19	0.5%
Lloyds Bank plc	1994	47,262	1.23	-0.32	0.86	1.34	1.5%
Lloyds Bank plc	1995	47,070	1.24	-0.49	0.77	1.54	3.6%
Lloyds Bank plc	1996	50,520	1.26	-0.56	0.73	1.59	4.9%
Lloyds TSB Group plc	1994	62,116	1.28	-0.03	0.98	1.03	0.0%
Lloyds TSB Group plc	1995	61,178	1.29	-0.14	0.93	1.13	0.3%

TABLE 7.7. Selected firm-level statistics: UK (cont'd)

BANK	YEAR	EMPL.	κ	λ	φ^l	φ^t	τ
Lloyds TSB Group plc	1996	68,787	1.31	-0.46	0.78	1.46	3.2%
Midland Bank Plc	1989	61,887	1.22	0.04	1.02	0.95	0.0%
Midland Bank Plc	1990	60,791	1.23	0.05	1.02	0.95	0.0%
Midland Bank Plc	1991	45,177	1.19	0.14	1.06	0.85	0.3%
Midland Bank Plc	1992	46,519	1.20	-0.11	0.96	1.13	0.2%
Midland Bank Plc	1993	45,861	1.21	-0.28	0.88	1.33	1.2%
Midland Bank Plc	1994	45,054	1.21	-0.52	0.78	1.64	3.9%
Midland Bank Plc	1995	45,126	1.22	-0.77	0.67	2.01	8.4%
National Westminster Bank Plc	1989	102,171	1.29	-0.14	0.96	1.19	0.2%
National Westminster Bank Plc	1990	105,274	1.31	-0.08	0.97	1.10	0.1%
National Westminster Bank Plc	1991	104,590	1.31	-0.07	0.98	1.09	0.1%
National Westminster Bank Plc	1992	104,183	1.33	-0.07	0.97	1.08	0.1%
National Westminster Bank Plc	1993	98,456	1.33	-0.25	0.90	1.28	0.8%
National Westminster Bank Plc	1994	96,800	1.33	-0.40	0.83	1.46	2.3%
National Westminster Bank Plc	1995	79,209	1.31	-0.49	0.78	1.55	3.6%
National Westminster Bank Plc	1996	88,573	1.35	-0.52	0.76	1.54	4.0%
Royal Bank of Scotland Group	1994	21,231	1.10	-0.31	0.84	1.34	1.6%
Royal Bank of Scotland Group	1995	21,459	1.12	-0.40	0.78	1.42	2.8%
Royal Bank of Scotland Group	1996	21,740	1.13	-0.60	0.67	1.64	6.1%
Royal Bank of Scotland plc	1994	21,231	1.12	0.18	1.11	0.85	0.5%
Royal Bank of Scotland plc	1995	21,459	1.14	0.18	1.12	0.86	0.6%
Royal Bank of Scotland plc	1996	21,957	1.16	0.12	1.08	0.91	0.2%
Standard Chartered Plc	1993	20,955	1.09	-0.12	0.94	1.13	0.2%
TSB Group plc	1989	30,897	1.12	0.08	1.03	0.91	0.1%
TSB Group plc	1990	30,848	1.12	0.09	1.04	0.90	0.1%
TSB Group plc	1991	29,877	1.12	0.05	1.02	0.94	0.0%
TSB Group plc	1992	22,785	1.10	0.12	1.06	0.88	0.3%
TSB Group plc	1993	21,256	1.10	-0.05	0.98	1.05	0.0%

TABLE 7.8. Selected firm-level statistics: US

BANK	YEAR	EMPL.	κ	λ	φ^l	φ^t	τ
Banc One Corporation	1992	30,933	1.15	0.38	1.19	0.67	2.4%
Banc One Corporation	1993	41,255	1.21	0.20	1.10	0.82	0.6%
Banc One Corporation	1994	42,730	1.22	0.10	1.05	0.91	0.2%
Banc One Corporation	1995	40,625	1.22	-0.12	0.94	1.11	0.2%
Bank of America Nat. Trust	1989	73,424	1.27	0.66	1.27	0.46	6.6%
Bank of America Nat. Trust	1990	70,820	1.27	0.54	1.22	0.54	4.4%
Bank of America Nat. Trust	1991	68,275	1.27	0.55	1.24	0.55	4.6%
Bank of America Nat. Trust	1992	60,536	1.26	0.51	1.24	0.59	4.1%
Bank of America Nat. Trust	1993	63,086	1.28	0.33	1.16	0.73	1.7%
Bank of America Nat. Trust	1994	61,172	1.28	0.14	1.07	0.88	0.3%
Bank of America Nat. Trust	1995	64,512	1.30	-0.09	0.95	1.08	0.1%
Bank of America Nat. Trust	1996	67,490	1.32	-0.16	0.91	1.14	0.4%
Bank of Boston Corporation	1995	20,823	1.11	-0.41	0.78	1.44	2.9%
Bank of New York	1989	20,179	1.05	0.12	1.05	0.85	0.2%
Bank of New York	1996	20,793	1.11	-1.03	0.51	2.41	15.8%
Bank of New York Co.	1993	20,615	1.09	-0.01	0.99	1.01	0.0%
Bank of New York Co.	1994	20,756	1.10	-0.25	0.87	1.26	1.0%
Bank of New York Co.	1995	21,194	1.11	-0.44	0.77	1.48	3.3%
Bankamerica Corporation	1992	80,804	1.30	0.45	1.20	0.63	3.1%
Bankamerica Corporation	1993	87,044	1.33	0.33	1.15	0.72	1.7%
Bankamerica Corporation	1994	88,871	1.34	0.14	1.07	0.88	0.3%
Bankamerica Corporation	1995	93,646	1.36	-0.02	0.99	1.02	0.0%
Bankers Trust Company	1990	32,124	1.11	-0.20	0.93	1.29	0.5%
Bankers Trust Company	1991	30,000	1.12	-0.09	0.96	1.12	0.1%
Bankers Trust Company	1992	29,763	1.13	-0.04	0.98	1.04	0.0%
Bankers Trust Company	1993	38,317	1.18	-0.23	0.90	1.26	0.8%
Bankers Trust Company	1994	29,721	1.18	0.38	1.23	0.71	2.5%
Bankers Trust Company	1995	28,994	1.16	-0.35	0.82	1.36	2.0%
Bankers Trust Company	1996	31,964	1.19	-0.60	0.70	1.65	5.7%
Bankers Trust New York Corp	1992	36,173	1.15	-0.24	0.91	1.30	0.8%
Bankers Trust New York Corp	1993	47,080	1.20	-0.52	0.80	1.73	3.7%

TABLE 7.8. Selected firm-level statistics: US (cont'd)

BANK	YEAR	EMPL.	κ	λ	φ^l	φ^t	τ
Bankers Trust New York Corp	1994	36,493	1.19	-0.25	0.88	1.27	1.0%
Bankers Trust New York Corp	1995	34,682	1.19	-0.28	0.86	1.28	1.3%
Chase Manhattan Bank NA	1989	45,828	1.18	0.24	1.09	0.74	0.8%
Chase Manhattan Bank NA	1990	45,325	1.19	0.34	1.14	0.67	1.7%
Chase Manhattan Bank NA	1991	42,050	1.18	0.10	1.04	0.89	0.2%
Chase Manhattan Bank NA	1992	40,828	1.18	0.02	1.01	0.98	0.0%
Chase Manhattan Bank NA	1993	44,066	1.22	0.37	1.19	0.70	2.2%
Chase Manhattan Bank NA	1994	50,915	1.24	-0.32	0.86	1.35	1.5%
Chase Manhattan Bank NA	1995	49,376	1.25	-0.32	0.85	1.32	1.6%
Chase Manhattan Corporation	1992	51,201	1.22	0.23	1.10	0.78	0.9%
Chase Manhattan Corporation	1993	52,576	1.25	0.37	1.18	0.70	2.2%
Chase Manhattan Corporation	1994	59,003	1.26	-0.19	0.91	1.20	0.6%
Chase Manhattan Corporation	1995	56,317	1.26	-0.37	0.83	1.39	2.1%
Chemical Bank	1989	26,112	1.10	0.42	1.18	0.59	2.9%
Chemical Bank	1990	24,561	1.10	0.34	1.15	0.66	1.9%
Chemical Bank	1991	24,408	1.11	0.64	1.33	0.49	6.9%
Chemical Bank	1992	48,381	1.22	0.29	1.13	0.74	1.3%
Chemical Bank	1993	46,472	1.22	0.23	1.11	0.80	0.8%
Chemical Bank	1994	46,335	1.24	0.17	1.09	0.85	0.5%
Chemical Bank	1995	44,548	1.24	-0.01	1.00	1.01	0.0%
Chemical Banking Corporation	1992	62,478	1.26	0.28	1.12	0.75	1.2%
Chemical Banking Corporation	1993	62,453	1.27	0.21	1.10	0.81	0.7%
Chemical Banking Corporation	1994	64,412	1.28	0.04	1.02	0.96	0.0%
Chemical Banking Corporation	1995	64,210	1.28	-0.43	0.81	1.46	2.7%
Citibank NA	1989	84,332	1.29	0.61	1.24	0.49	5.5%
Citibank NA	1990	96,899	1.31	0.51	1.20	0.56	3.8%
Citibank NA	1991	95,982	1.32	0.43	1.17	0.62	2.7%
Citibank NA	1992	86,443	1.31	0.46	1.20	0.63	3.2%
Citibank NA	1993	87,322	1.33	0.41	1.19	0.68	2.6%
Citibank NA	1994	88,140	1.34	0.26	1.13	0.79	1.0%
Citibank NA	1995	92,253	1.36	0.05	1.03	0.95	0.0%

TABLE 7.8. Selected firm-level statistics: US (cont'd)

BANK	YEAR	EMPL.	κ	λ	φ^l	φ^t	τ
Citibank NA	1996	96,557	1.38	-0.02	0.99	1.02	0.0%
Citicorp	1992	127,855	1.37	0.39	1.16	0.67	2.2%
Citicorp	1993	131,616	1.39	0.25	1.11	0.78	0.9%
Citicorp	1994	125,827	1.39	0.09	1.04	0.92	0.1%
Citicorp	1995	132,924	1.41	-0.11	0.95	1.10	0.2%
First Chicago Corporation	1989	20,921	1.07	0.43	1.19	0.58	3.0%
First Chicago Corporation	1990	20,122	1.07	0.52	1.25	0.54	4.5%
First Chicago Corporation	1991	20,214	1.08	0.49	1.24	0.58	4.0%
First Chicago Corporation	1993	21,628	1.10	0.13	1.07	0.88	0.3%
First Chicago Corporation	1994	39,027	1.20	-0.09	0.96	1.08	0.1%
First Chicago Corporation	1995	39,278	1.22	-0.12	0.94	1.11	0.2%
First Chicago NBD Corp	1995	39,278	1.22	-0.12	0.94	1.11	0.2%
First Chicago NBD Corp	1996	37,760	1.22	-0.44	0.77	1.44	3.2%
First Interstate Bancorp	1992	27,529	1.13	0.25	1.12	0.77	1.0%
First Interstate Bancorp	1993	24,692	1.12	0.07	1.03	0.94	0.1%
First Interstate Bancorp	1994	26,310	1.14	-0.10	0.95	1.10	0.2%
First Interstate Bancorp	1995	24,630	1.15	-0.18	0.90	1.17	0.6%
First Union Corporation	1992	22,714	1.10	0.30	1.15	0.73	1.5%
First Union Corporation	1993	29,276	1.15	0.16	1.08	0.85	0.4%
First Union Corporation	1994	31,353	1.17	-0.04	0.98	1.04	0.0%
First Union Corporation	1995	33,962	1.19	-0.19	0.90	1.18	0.6%
Fleet Financial Group	1992	27,236	1.14	0.45	1.23	0.62	3.4%
Fleet Financial Group	1993	26,111	1.14	0.30	1.16	0.75	1.5%
Fleet Financial Group	1994	23,363	1.13	0.03	1.02	0.97	0.0%
Fleet Financial Group	1995	33,939	1.21	0.24	1.15	0.82	1.0%
KeyCorp	1994	24,654	1.14	0.11	1.06	0.90	0.2%
KeyCorp	1995	26,325	1.16	-0.17	0.90	1.16	0.5%
Mellon Bank Corporation	1994	23,290	1.14	0.27	1.16	0.78	1.3%
Mellon Bank Corporation	1995	22,216	1.13	-0.13	0.93	1.12	0.3%
Morgan Guaranty Trust NY	1989	28,461	1.10	0.03	1.01	0.96	0.0%
Morgan Guaranty Trust NY	1990	29,350	1.10	-0.23	0.92	1.36	0.7%

TABLE 7.8. Selected firm-level statistics: US (cont'd)

BANK	YEAR	EMPL.	κ	λ	φ^i	φ^t	τ
Morgan Guaranty Trust NY	1991	32,544	1.14	0.06	1.03	0.93	0.1%
Morgan Guaranty Trust NY	1992	35,641	1.15	-0.26	0.90	1.33	1.0%
Morgan Guaranty Trust NY	1993	40,597	1.19	-0.05	0.98	1.05	0.0%
Morgan Guaranty Trust NY	1994	36,225	1.19	-0.18	0.91	1.18	0.5%
Morgan Guaranty Trust NY	1995	39,092	1.21	-0.24	0.88	1.23	0.9%
Morgan Guaranty Trust NY	1996	33,778	1.21	-0.10	0.94	1.08	0.2%
NationsBank Corporation	1992	48,328	1.22	0.42	1.20	0.65	2.8%
NationsBank Corporation	1993	48,194	1.23	0.33	1.16	0.73	1.8%
NationsBank Corporation	1994	56,299	1.26	0.08	1.04	0.93	0.1%
NationsBank Corporation	1995	57,803	1.28	-0.08	0.96	1.08	0.1%
Nationsbank of NC	1995	21,612	1.13	0.03	1.02	0.97	0.0%
Nationsbank of NC	1996	20,816	1.14	-0.02	0.99	1.01	0.0%
NBD Bancorp	1995	39,278	1.22	-0.11	0.94	1.10	0.2%
Norwest Corporation	1992	28,912	1.14	0.26	1.13	0.76	1.1%
Norwest Corporation	1993	35,886	1.18	0.02	1.01	0.98	0.0%
Norwest Corporation	1994	38,345	1.20	-0.14	0.93	1.14	0.3%
Norwest Corporation	1995	40,509	1.22	-0.27	0.86	1.27	1.2%
PNC Bancorp, Inc.	1995	23,191	1.15	0.08	1.05	0.94	0.1%
PNC Bank Corp.	1994	20,488	1.11	-0.03	0.98	1.03	0.0%
PNC Bank Corp.	1995	24,932	1.15	0.02	1.01	0.98	0.0%
PNC Financial Corp.	1994	20,488	1.11	-0.03	0.98	1.03	0.0%
PNC Financial Corp.	1995	24,955	1.15	0.02	1.01	0.98	0.0%
Wells Fargo Bank NA	1989	23,177	1.09	0.56	1.25	0.50	5.1%
Wells Fargo Bank NA	1990	23,363	1.09	0.46	1.21	0.58	3.5%
Wells Fargo Bank NA	1991	23,401	1.11	0.61	1.31	0.51	6.1%
Wells Fargo Bank NA	1992	23,752	1.12	0.47	1.25	0.62	3.7%
Wells Fargo Bank NA	1993	24,971	1.13	0.28	1.15	0.76	1.4%
Wells Fargo Bank NA	1994	24,751	1.14	0.04	1.02	0.97	0.0%
Wells Fargo Bank NA	1995	22,889	1.14	0.04	1.03	0.96	0.0%
Wells Fargo Bank NA	1996	39,795	1.25	0.17	1.11	0.87	0.5%

Index